Dred Scott

The Inside Story

David T. Hardy

REPORT

OF

THE DECISION

OF THE

SUPREME COURT OF THE UNITED STATES,

AND THE

OPINIONS OF THE JUDGES THEREOF,

IN THE CASE OF

DRED SCOTT

VERSUS

JOHN F. A. SANDFORD.

DECEMBER TERM, 1856.

BY BENJAMIN C. HOWARD,
FROM THE NINETEENTH VOLUME OF HOWARD'S REPORTS.

WASHINGTON:
CORNELIUS WENDELL, PRINTER.
1857.

Table of Contents

Introduction

A political system at the breaking point. A Chief Justice driven to break the rules of his own Court. A fellow Justice who has his eye on the presidency. Four more Justices who are secretly conniving with the President, with the aim of striking down an act of Congress. A supposed slaveowner, who didn't own slaves. An abolitionist, who did. A former Attorney General, actively falsifying evidence. A country on the brink of civil war…

Welcome to *Dred Scott v. John F. A. Sandford*, the 1857 Supreme Court ruling that changed the course of a nation.

Not that anyone involved foresaw that result. The slave, Dred Scott, began with an ordinary "freedom suit," a state lawsuit which should have been an easy win. Fifteen years later, he ended with a federal lawsuit that lost in the Supreme Court, in a ruling that struck down as unconstitutional all restrictions on slavery in the territories. That decision brought about the rise of Lincoln and the fracture of the Democratic Party.

Yet, change any one of a number of circumstances, and *Dred Scott v. John F. A. Sandford* would never have happened. If Dred Scott or his wife had never heard of Missouri "freedom suits," if the Missouri Supreme Court had adhered to its past rulings and declared his family free under state law, if Scott's attorney had realized that he stood no chance before the U.S. Supreme Court, if a New York businessman had not agreed to pose as Dred Scott's owner, if the Supreme Court had kept with its original plan and ruled without striking down the Missouri Compromise …

Then Abraham Lincoln might be a footnote in history, an upstart frontier politician who (if he even won the nomination) lost to President Stephen Douglas, the Civil War might never have occurred (at least not when and how it did), and the 13th, 14th and 15th Amendments to the Constitution, which abolished slavery, established that black Americans were citizens and voters, and bound state governments to provide "due process of law" and "equal protection of the laws," might never have been drafted.

In sectional terms, the Civil War led to a Northern/Midwestern congressional monopoly, which profoundly changed the evolving nation. The 1862 Homestead Act, which offered farmers free land, and the transcontinental railroad, whose construction begun in 1863, meant that the Great Plains would be filled by free farmers, many of them immigrants, with the result that both our population and our land under cultivation doubled in thirty years.

In short, without Dred Scott the United States would be a different place with a radically different history. It might not even be a superpower. In 1857, when the Dred Scott decision was handed down, the United States had an army of 12,000 men – Belgium had an army twice as large. The United States Navy had 42 ships afloat, all wooden and most outdated. Eight years later, in 1865, the United States Army had over a million men in arms, and its Navy was the second-largest on the planet, with the world's largest force of ironclads. The U.S. was not yet a superpower, but well on its way to becoming one.

Dred and Harriett Scotts' quest for freedom thus marks a watershed in history, an event that took a nation heading toward one destiny and set it on the path to quite a different one. Given that the nation in question was the United States, the Scotts' quest was a significant event in world history as well.

All in all, quite a set of consequences for an elderly slave's bid for freedom, represented by an attorney who couldn't count votes.

Frank Leslie's Illustrated Newspaper had a circulation of over 100,000. In June, 1857, it gave the Scott family front-page coverage.

I
March 6, 1857

Roger Brooke Taney, fifth Chief Justice of the United States Supreme Court, arranged his papers and looked out upon the crowd that filled the small courtroom in the Capitol. Senators, Congressmen, some reporters – for once, it took real power to get a place in the room.

He had been old, 59, for a judicial nominee, when Andrew Jackson named him to the post. 1836, the year of the Alamo, the year that James Madison, the last of founders, died. Twenty-one years later, Taney was still alive, still sat at the center of the Court's bench.

Slavery was the issue of the ruling he would announce today, and his own thinking on the subject had changed greatly over his long life. As a young man he had inherited slaves, and promptly freed them, paying pensions to those too old to support themselves. He had successfully defended a Maryland minister accused of preaching an anti-slavery sermon to an audience that included slaves. In his argument to the jury he invoked the anti-slavery writings of Jefferson and other founding fathers, and challenged the court to convict the minister for statements that were milder than these thoughts. His passionate conclusion termed slavery an "evil" and a "blot on our national character," and called for its gradual termination, a day when "we can point without a blush to the language held in the Declaration of Independence."[1]

Four decades had passed since that oration, and Taney's thinking had changed; his transition mirrored the national experience. The slave issue had increasingly become a sectional one, North versus South, and the South increasingly grew defensive. The conflict was not focused on slavery where it existed – true abolitionists were a tiny minority in those days – but on where slavery might spread, in the vast territories to the west. If a sufficient number of territories allowed slavery, when they became slave states they would keep the South secure in its rough Senate parity. If they became free territories and then free states, the slave interest would lose the Senate, as it had long since lost the House.

It was a clash of dreams, not of economics. The Midwest shared the South's economic interests – rural, agrarian, exporting economies

– but remained solidly anti-slavery. The clash was over how to populate the Great Plains and the West. In one dream, they would be filled by European immigrants, at the time largely Irish and German, offered free government land. In the other, they would be filled with plantations, with its people (the free population, anyway) preserving the Anglo-American culture of the last century. In a few years, men would fight and die over which dream would become a reality.

None of this Chief Justice Taney could foresee, on that sunny day in March 1857. If anything, he saw the opinion he would read as forestalling that very conflict. If Congress had no constitutional power to restrict slavery in the territories, the main political issue that was dividing the country would vanish. A national politician would have no reason to run on the slavery issue if he had no power over the subject. The slavery issue would swiftly vanish, and the country would be as it was when Taney was a young lawyer, accepting slavery while hoping for its eventual, gradual, end.

The Chief Justice's face had always been solemn, but today it showed the deep marks of tragedy. His family had long vacationed at Old Point Lookout, a beach location at the tip of the Virginia Peninsula. In summer 1855, less than two years before, his youngest daughter Alice had asked to vacation with friends going to Rhode Island. She or they referred to it as a healthier summer location, and Taney responded with irritation: "I have not the slightest confidence in the superior health of Newport over Old Point, and look upon it as nothing more than that unfortunate feeling of inferiority in the South, which believes everything in the North to be superior to what we have."[2]

It was pleasant but cool vacation, marred by reports of a Yellow Fever epidemic in New Orleans that was spreading to the north and east. It soon reached Norfolk, right across the bay from Old Point Comfort. The Taneys hoped that it would end there. It didn't. On two successive days, Yellow Fever claimed the life of Alice, and of Taney's wife Anne.[3] Taney's friends described him as guilt-stricken and as bawling like a baby.

Perhaps guilt played some role in what Taney set out to do this March morning, unsettling his mind, making him miss the consequences of his plan. He would lead off, reading a lengthy opinion that would rock Washington. Describing the facts would be simple. A Missouri man, Dred Scott, had sued a New Yorker, John

Sanford, in federal court, under a provision of the Constitution that allowed federal courts to judge claims between citizens of different states. Scott contended that Sanford held him in slavery when actually he was a free man, since he had been voluntarily taken into a free state and a territory where slavery was illegal under the Missouri Compromise. Since he had been freed by the terms of that 1820 Congressional act, he remained free when he returned to Missouri.

Taney's opinion would reject that claim. He would start off by ruling that federal courts had no jurisdiction to hear Dred Scott's case. The case had been based upon "diversity jurisdiction," where a citizen of one state can go into federal court to sue a citizen of a different state. Taney would rule that, even if he were a free man, Dred Scott was not a citizen, because the framers of the Constitution had never intended for free blacks to be citizens. Thus the suit was not between citizens of different states, and a federal court could not accept it.

That was not the bombshell, however. Taney would go on to rule that the Missouri Compromise had been unconstitutional! Congress had no legal power to restrict slavery in the territories. The political battles of the last forty years, the battle even now occurred in Kansas, had been over a nullity.

That would be earthshaking in itself. But Taney would add another section equally startling. There was an alternative to having Congress decide whether a territory would be free or slave: let the people of the territory decide for themselves, through their elected legislature. This approach, "popular sovereignty," had been espoused by many moderate pro-slavery figures, including incoming President James Buchanan and Lincoln's future rival Stephen Douglas.

But, having taken down Congressional powers to restrict slavery, Taney's opinion would take down popular sovereignty as well. Since territorial governments had only the powers Congress gave them, and Congress had no power to restrict slavery, territorial governments were likewise unable to restrict slavery.

The import of the rule was that there was no longer any such thing as a free territory, at a time when territories made up the majority of the U.S. landmass. Only when a territory became a state would it be able to ban slavery, and by then territories with climates suitable for slavery would have enough slave owners to make this impossible. Taney's opinion would thus settle the territorial question solidly in favor of human slavery.

Taney looked to his right. Next to him sat the senior Associate Justice, John McLean of Ohio, one of the two dissenters from today's ruling, two Justices who would speak tomorrow in opposition to it. Taney had reason to view McLean with distrust. Despite his age (in five days he would turn 80) McLean harbored presidential ambitions. In the 1856 Republican Convention, he had taken second place, with 190 ballots, or over a third of those cast. It was an impressive showing, particularly since his sponsor had betrayed him by announcing he was withdrawing McLean's name from consideration.[4] McLean would try again, Taney knew, and tomorrow's dissent would be his first campaign speech.

Taney was perhaps amused by an irony. As candidate, McLean had some political baggage: he'd twice voted to uphold the Fugitive Slave Act, a draconian measure meant to ensure the capture of escaped slaves. He'd tried to offset that by publishing a newspaper article arguing that Congress had no power to *impose* slavery on a territory, and since a territorial legislature had only the power Congress could give it, it likewise could not create a slave territory.[5] Taney would borrow McLean's argument and turn it upon him.

Beyond McLean sat Justice John Catron, a Tennessean and slave owner, a large and outspoken man who was fond of dueling. That probably raised him in the eyes of his fellow duelist Andrew Jackson, who appointed him to the Court.

(Washington insiders knew that Justice Catron's one descendant was James P. Thomas, born to a slave mother. Thomas ran a barber shop near the Tennessee state capitol; when he was freed in 1851 he had enough influence to get a legislative exemption from laws that required freed slaves to leave the state. He later moved to St. Louis where he became one of the wealthiest men in the city).[6]

Catron would predictably concur in Taney's ruling, although differing with its reasoning. He would opine that Congress did have general power over slavery in the territories, but that power was curtailed by the treaty that carried out the Louisiana Purchase, and which guaranteed the property rights of residents in those lands.

Beyond Catron sat Justice Samuel Nelson, a New Yorker, nominated by President Tyler after the Senate had rejected four of Tyler's nominees in a row. Nelson, like Tyler, was a Democrat, and the Senate was controlled by their rivals the Whigs, but Nelson's record of impartiality had been sufficient for him to gain confirmation.

On the Supreme Court, Nelson was famous for writing "narrow" opinions, deciding a case on the narrowest grounds possible. Weeks before, he had been Taney's first choice as author of today's opinion. Nelson thought it could be decided on the ground that a person's status, slave or free, was governed by the law of the jurisdiction in which the person resided. Yes, a slave whose master takes him into a free state becomes free, but if he returns to a slave state he reverts to being a slave. Dred Scott's mistake had been returning to slave state Missouri. That ruling would have been unlikely to stir much controversy.

Then Justices McLean and Curtis disclosed that they were writing broad dissents that would support Congressional power over slavery in the territories, and Taney decided to write the opinion himself, and reach that issue. Taney knew that Nelson would write a separate opinion, concurring in the majority ruling, on the narrow ground for which he had originally argued. That meant he would join in the ruling but not in its striking down Congressional power over the territories.

At the far end of the bench to his right sat Justice Benjamin Robbins Curtis, of Massachusetts. He was the other dissenting vote, and likely the more dangerous one. Curtis was a better writer and clearer legal thinker than McLean. If Taney's opinion had holes in it, Curtis was the man to find them.

Taney may have resented Curtis' opposition all the more because Curtis was both young (47) and the second-most junior Justice, with only five years on this bench. After the dissents were read, the normally courteous Taney would become singularly rude toward Curtis.

To Taney's immediate left was Justice James Moore Wayne, a Georgian, and second most senior Associate Justice. Wayne was firmly pro-slavery and would concur in Taney's opinion.

To Wayne's left sat Justice Peter Daniel, a tall and strongly-built Virginian. Taney was not the only Justice affected by family tragedy: only two months before, Daniel's wife Elizabeth had been fatally burned when, at a holiday party, a candle set fire to her dress.

Daniel was a staunch supporter of slavery and opponent of expanded federal powers, and he would write a concurrence. This was unusual for him – when he did not dissent, as he often did, he usually just joined the majority opinion. His concurrence would suggest that Congress lacked power over slavery in the territories, and that the case should have been dismissed for lack of jurisdiction.

Past Daniel sat Justice Robert Grier, from Pennsylvania. In the slang of the day, Grier was a "doughface," a northerner strongly sympathetic to slavery. As a trial judge, he had denounced abolitionists as "infuriated fanatics and unprincipled demagogues" who went against "the Constitution, laws, and the Bible."[7]

Taney knew that Grier had been in secret correspondence with his friend President James Buchanan about the case, filling Buchanan in on the Court's deliberations and its voting, while Buchanan lobbied him to join the Court's opinion and to ensure it was a broad one – which in context meant striking down Congressional power over slavery in the territories. Grier had even coached Buchanan on how to refer to the case in his inaugural address. Taney also knew that Buchanan hadn't invented the idea of lobbying Grier; Justice Catron had asked Buchanan to do it, so that the vote against the Missouri Compromise would include at least one northerner.

The President conspiring with Justices of the Supreme Court, with an eye to striking down a Congressional enactment.... Chief Justice Taney was a principled man; that he would accept such gross impropriety is an indication of how strongly he felt about the issue now before him.

Grier's concurring opinion would be the shortest of them all, a single paragraph. He would agree with Nelson that a slave taken to a free state reverted to slave status upon returning to a slave state, and since a slave could not be a citizen the Court had no jurisdiction. He would add that he agreed with Taney on the issue of the Missouri Compromise and congressional power over slavery.

To Grier's left sat Justice John Archibald Campbell, of Alabama. Young, a mere 46, he was considered a moderate on slavery. He was a slaveowner, but had published articles calling for a gradual end to slavery, and freed many of his own slaves as a start. He had a good mind and wrote well; he would be a useful ally. Taney knew he would write a concurrence joining in Taney's opinion.

At the end, the vote would stand 7-2 overall, and 6-3 on striking down Congressional power over territorial slavery. Decisive majorities, and with one northern Justice joining in both, not ones that could be attributed simply to slave-state Justices voting for slavery.

Weak and in poor health, Taney had steeled himself for the reading. He would have to try to project his faltering voice through the room as for two hours. "This case has been twice argued," he began.

> *After the argument at the last term, differences of opinion were found to exist among the members of the court, and as the questions in controversy are of the highest importance, and the court was at that time much pressed by the ordinary business of the term, it was deemed advisable to continue the case and direct a re-argument on some of the points in order that we might have an opportunity of giving to the whole subject a more deliberate consideration. It has accordingly been again argued by counsel, and considered by the court; and I now proceed to deliver its opinion.*

History had reached a turning point, and the opinion the ancient Chief Justice was reading would determine its path. It would not be the path he intended.

Four years later, almost to the day, Justice Taney would again climb the steps of the Capitol. This time, it would be to swear in Abraham Lincoln as President of the United States.

II
A Very Well-Travelled Slave

Of the protagonist of this tale, we know regrettably little. In 1856 Dred Scott was one of St. Louis' 2,500 or so slaves; in 1857 he briefly held national fame; in 1858, he was dead of tuberculosis. We do not know the year of his birth, or his parents' names. For that matter, until recently we did not even know his real name. Only in 2009 did historian Lea VanderVelde discover military records showing that his first name was Etheldred;[8] he understandably chose to go by the nickname of Dred.

Most of what we know of the Scott family's personalities is taken from *Frank Leslie's Illustrated Newspaper*, a popular national newspaper of the time. Its June 27, 1857 issue reported interviews with the Scott family. Dred was described as "a pure-blooded African, perhaps fifty years of age, with a shrewd, intelligent, good-natured face, of rather light frame, being not more than five feet, six inches high." His wife Harriett they described as "a smart, tidy-looking negress, perhaps thirty years of age," who was ironing clothes with her daughters. She apparently wore the pants in the family: the correspondent referred to her as "the legitimate owner of Dred." She seems to have interested the writer as much as Dred did: she is described as "neat, industrious, and devotedly attached to her husband and children, an acceptable member of the church, and would evidently be satisfied with obscurity and repose."

The article closed with an appraisal of her husband: "Dred, although illiterate, is not ignorant. He has travelled considerably and has improved his stock of strong common sense by much information picked up in his journeyings."

Yes, one thing in Scott's life is clear: he was well-travelled, and his travels would play a role in his suits for freedom.

First moves: Virginia to Alabama to St. Louis

Dred Scott was born sometime in the period 1790-1799, in southeastern Virginia, as a slave to the Peter Blow family. In 1818, he moved with the Blows to a new farm near Huntsville, Alabama. In

1830, he again moved with them to St. Louis, Missouri, as they gave up farming and began operating a boarding house.

Scott would soon be sold, but his ties to the Blow family would continue. Peter's son, Taylor Blow, remained Dred's close friend, and supported him in his litigation. The friendship went beyond the grave. When the cemetery that first held Scott's remains closed, Blow had his remains moved to his own plot in another cemetery.[9] Perhaps Dred became a father figure after Blow was orphaned in his teens.[10] In his *Frank Leslie's Illustrated Newspaper* interview, Scott referred to Taylor Blow as one of "them boys he was brought up with."

From Missouri (a slave state) to Illinois (a free state)

Aged in his 30s, Scott had already moved 900 miles, a considerable distance when movement was by horse or foot. But his travels were just beginning. Sometime in the early 1830s Peter Blow sold Scott to a St. Louis army surgeon named John Emerson. Prof. VanderVelde recently discovered that Emerson bought Scott just before Emerson's 1833 departure on assignment to Fort Armstrong, in the free state of Illinois. She also found that Emerson may have been planning to use Scott to exploit a loophole in Army regulations, under which a second lieutenant drew $30 a month salary, plus an allowance of $14.50 for a servant. Emerson and three lieutenants each claimed Scott as their servant, and each collected the allowance. The four were thus able to split $58 a month for Scott's services, nearly a 50% boost in their compensation.[11] (We may hope they gave Dred a piece of the action).

Illinois to Wisconsin Territory (a free territory); the Scotts' marriage

Then as now, military personnel were kept on the move. Fort Armstrong's original purpose had been to establish an American presence on the frontier and to control movement on the Mississippi; it later served as a major base during the Black Hawk War of 1832. By the time Emerson and Scott arrived in 1833, its garrison had been reduced to about a hundred men. In 1836 the Army decided to withdraw its garrison entirely, and Dr. Emerson drew a new assignment. It was to Fort Snelling, in the Wisconsin Territory, near today's Minneapolis, Minnesota.

The latest move took Scott out of a free state into a free territory.

Under the 1820 Missouri Compromise, Congress had agreed to admit Missouri as a slave state, and in return that slavery would otherwise be forbidden in territories above the latitude of 36.5 degrees (the northern border of what are now Arkansas and Tennessee). Fort Snelling was over six hundred miles into the "free" zone. This, too, would factor into Scott's eventual lawsuit.

Fort Snelling was a much larger post than Fort Armstrong had been, and its Indian Agent and sometimes acting commander was a Virginian, Major Lawrence Taliaferro. A career officer, Taliaferro performed his duties with exceptional honor. One chieftain called him "no sugar in mouth" for his candor. The diary he kept reflects concerns that he would be replaced by someone who "can more easily be bribed or threatened into silence and acquiescence in the plans on foot to cheat & destroy the Indians." The local tribes sold furs to the American Fur Company, which Taliaferro knew was guilty of sharp practices.

Taliaferro had a direct impact on Dred Scott's life. One of Taliaferro's servants (the ambiguity of that term is useful here, as will be shown) was Harriet Robinson, and she and Dred Scott soon became spouses.

Although the Scott's attorneys would never argue the point, the wedding ceremony had major legal significance. Marriage is, in the civil law, a contract, and slaves had no legal capacity to make a contract.

Both Dr. Emerson and Major Taliaferro knew of the wedding. Indeed, Major Taliaferro, acting in his capacity as Indian Agent (the closest thing to a Justice of the Peace in the area), personally performed the wedding ceremony! In an autobiography Taliaferro authored three decades later, he wrote of himself in the third person:

In order to enforce morality as far as practicable, being the highest officer at the post, he induced many traders with growing Indian families to legitimize their children by marriage. There being no minister in the country, he officiated as a justice of the peace, and united many, among them was Oliver Cratte to Miss Graham, James Wells to Miss Graham, daughters of Duncan Graham: Alpheus R. French to Mary Henry, of Ohio, closing with the union of Dred Scott with Harriet Robinson — my servant girl, which I gave him.[12]

He "gave" her to *Dred Scott*, as a father might "give" a bride. He did not, as the Supreme Court would later be incorrectly told, *sell* her to *Dr. Emerson*. In his unpublished autobiography, Taliaferro adds that "The agent [that is, himself] in after years gave freedom to all his slaves." Among his papers held by the Minnesota Historical Society is his handwritten list of "slaves I freed from slavery 1839-43," and on it appears the name "Harriett."[13]

The marriage would seem persuasive evidence that certainly Major Taliaferro, and probably Dr. Emerson, regarded the couple as free, but, as noted, their future attorneys would never argue the point.

Life at Fort Snelling was hard, even for a frontier outpost. The Great Plains were in a prolonged cold spell, coming at the end of the Little Ice Age. The Mississippi was frozen solid from November 21, 1835 until April 7, 1836, and during this time the fort was cut off from the boats that would bring supplies and move passengers. In February, 1836, temperatures fell to -24, with over four feet of snow accumulation. Snow would still be falling in late April.[14]

From Wisconsin Territory back to Missouri (a slave state); Dr. Emerson's marriage

It was long known that Dr. Emerson left Fort Snelling – he married in Louisiana in 1838 and thereafter was located in St. Louis - while the Scotts remained behind at Fort Snelling until 1840. Historians assumed that Dr. Emerson left Fort Snelling, letting the Scotts stay behind for unknown reasons, then sent for them to join him, travelling on their own. But letters from him have been found as late as March, 1840, giving his location as Fort Snelling.[15] Prof. Vandervelde found the answer in military records. When Emerson departed Fort Snelling in October 1838, the last river boat had come and gone; he had to travel by canoe, and there was no room for the Scotts to accompany him. He thereafter served in Louisiana and St. Louis, then pestered the military into returning him to Ft. Snelling.[16] From there, he travelled with the Scotts to St. Louis in 1840.

But this portion of Dr. Emerson's travels were of far less importance than his marriage, since his spouse would outlive him and play a more important role in the Scotts' future. Emerson married Eliza Irene Sanford, who preferred to be known as Irene. Irene was one of seven children; her brother, John Sanford, would play his own role in the Scotts' lawsuit.

Dr. Emerson had a few years in St. Louis with his new bride. Then he was ordered to Florida, where the Army was fighting the Seminoles. With the end of the Second Seminole War in 1842,[17] the Army decided to downsize and Dr. Emerson (who had secured his numerous transfers by pleading his poor health) found himself discharged from service. He tried and failed to establish himself in private practice in St. Louis, and decided to head back to the frontier.

Emerson had a major competitive advantage over other doctors in the west: he actually had an M.D., a rarity among frontier physicians. To take advantage of it, he relocated to Davenport, Iowa Territory, where he had long owned land, and began to build a house on one parcel. In May, 1843, he ran advertisements in the *Davenport Gazette*, offering his services and giving his location as a hotel.

He was not to have luck in Davenport. In late December 1843, he died there. His death certificate listed the cause of death as "quick consumption" – given medicine of the time, all we can assume is that it was some manner of pulmonary ailment.

In the last few days of his life Dr. Emerson sold two parcels of realty and wrote out his will. By it, he left his medical books to his brother and all other property he left to his wife Irene "for & during the term of her natural life," and "immediately after her decease, I give & devise the same to my daughter Henrietta Sanford Emerson…" He nominated his brother-in-law, John Sanford, and a local friend, George L. Davenport, to be the will's executors. Sanford never qualified as executor; with Davenport at the scene he was not necessary.

By 1840, then, Dred Scott had lived for three years in Illinois, whose constitution provided that "Neither slavery nor involuntary servitude shall hereafter be introduced into the State, otherwise than for the punishment of crimes," and that *"any violation of this article shall effect the emancipation of such person from his obligation to service."*[18] He and Harriet had then spent four years at Fort Snelling, where slavery was forbidden by the Missouri Compromise, which provided that in northern territories, "slavery was shall be, and is hereby, forever prohibited."[19] Their first daughter, Eliza, had been born in Missouri Compromise territory, on the steamship as they returned to St. Louis.

The significance of the Scotts' travels would not be noted for over a decade. They lived in St. Louis and apparently regarded themselves as slaves of Irene Emerson, the doctor's widow. While there, Harriet bore a second daughter, Lizzie.

Then something happened, something that made the Scotts sue for their freedom. We will probably never know what it was: any witnesses are long dead, and no written records of its occurrence exist.[20] But it made Dred and Harriet Scott's lives a turning point of American history.

III
The Scotts' State "Freedom Suit"

We know very little about our main protagonists over the next few years, beyond the facts that Mrs. Emerson lived with her father, Alexander Sanford, at his plantation outside St. Louis, while the Scotts lived in the city, Dred working as a laborer and Harriet as a laundress. Beyond this there is only speculation and probable myth.

Slavery in St. Louis had by then taken on some distinctive and unusual features. Of the city's 80,000 inhabitants, only around 2,500 were slaves. There was also a growing population of just under 1,400 free blacks.[21] Some of the latter had become so prosperous that in 1858 author Cyprian Clamorgan documented them in a gossipy book, *The Colored Aristocracy of St. Louis*.[22] (One of his more interesting subjects was Pelagie Rutgers, a former slave who purchased her freedom for $3, invested in real estate, and in 1858 owned a mansion and an estate worth $500,000, or fifteen million dollars in modern money).

Within the city, slavery was on the wane; St. Louis had been flooded by German and Irish immigrants looking for work, which drove wages down and made slavery less economical. The custom grew of "hiring out" slaves, letting someone else pay the owner for the slaves' labor, and at times slaves hired themselves out, in return for getting to keep a part of the proceeds. Urban slaves could also hire out in their spare time (by custom they had Sunday and often part of Saturday off), and keep those earnings. Dred and Harriet may have put in quite a bit of overtime; Dred later said that he had offered Mrs. Emerson $300 (over a year's wages for a free laborer) for his freedom, but was refused.

(It may be helpful at this point to pretend you are in an alternate reality. In this particular world, strange as it may seem, a person can have a deed to another human being (the deed being quitclaim or coming with a warranty that the person really is a slave), people can be bought, sold, and leased. A slave can buy himself, thereby becoming free (but needing a license to stay in the state), he can also lease himself out and keep a finder's fee, and have a second job for his own profit.[23] Don't try to understand, just think of it as an alternative reality sci-fi novel – even though it once *was* reality).

What were "freedom suits"?

This alternative reality would need a legal system able to deal with the situation where a supposed slave contends that he is actually free, a person rather than property. Louisiana devoted an entire chapter of its statutes to dealing with the issue.[24] The chapter began in a straightforward manner:

Section 1. Any person held in slavery may petition the circuit court, or judge thereof, in vacation, for leave to sue, as a poor person, in order to establish his right to freedom, and shall state in his petition the ground on which his claim to freedom is founded.

The statute provided that if the judge found sufficient reason to sue, he should allow the lawsuit, and issue an order that the purported slave have "reasonable liberty to attend his counsel and the court, as occasion may require; that he not be removed out of the jurisdiction of the court, that he not be subject to any severity on account of his application for freedom." If the petitioner was not able to post a bond to cover court costs should he lose, the sheriff was to "hire him out to the best advantage," retain and invest the funds, and at the end of the case pay them to whoever won. The statute also specified that the lawsuit would take the form of "an action of trespass for false imprisonment." (Trespass was the common law equivalent of what today would be called "personal injury" lawsuits).

Such "freedom suits" were not a rarity; researchers have found over 300 freedom suits filed in the St. Louis courts.[25] The odds of the alleged slave winning were a bit under 50%.

The Scotts' grounds for suit were simple: Dr. Emerson had taken them into a free state and a free territory, and in particular Illinois, where (as we have seen) the state constitution not only forbade slavery, but provided that any slaves brought into the state automatically became free. The Scotts were thus freed, and remained so on their return to slave state Missouri.

Their argument was widely accepted. Courts had settled what happened when a master took a slave into a free state via comity, a matter of a court voluntarily showing respect for another state's laws. The compromise reached was essentially: (1) if the slave was only taken to a free state for a short time, a "sojourn," he remained a slave, and free state courts would recognize this, but (2) if the visit lasted longer than this, the slave was freed, and slave state courts would accept this. The length of a "sojourn" was not clearly defined, but was generally understood to be days or weeks rather than months.

By those standards, the Scotts were looking at a sure win. They had spent *years* in free states or territories. The Missouri Supreme Court had long accepted that, via comity, residence in a free state or territory made a slave free. In 1824, it ruled that a slave taken to the free Northwest Territory for a few years was free upon her return to Missouri, and it repeated this doctrine in 1828, 1827, 1830, 1833, 1834, 1836, 1837, 1844 and 1845.[26] The 1836 ruling, in particular, matched the Scotts' situation; the slaveowner had been an Army officer, assigned to Fort Snelling. The officer argued that he had not gone to free territory of his own will, but by command of his superiors. The Missouri Supreme Court easily disposed of that claim: "though it be that the officer was bound to remain where he did, during all the time he was there, yet no authority of law or the government compelled him to keep the plaintiff there as a slave."

The Scotts file a freedom suit against Irene Emerson

The Scotts and their attorneys thus had reason to be optimistic when, in April, 1846, they filed two freedom suits (one for Dred and one for Harriet) in the Circuit Court for St. Louis County. The suits named Irene Emerson as defendant, and plead that she had held them as slaves. The complaints also alleged that Irene had "beat, bruised, and ill-treated him, the said plaintiff, and kept and detained him in prison...."[27]

The allegations do not suggest that Mrs. Emerson was a brawler; Scott's attorney appears to have been using old boilerplate. The 1845 Missouri Revised Statutes required only that "[t]he action to be brought under the leave given, shall be an action of trespass for false imprisonment,"[28] but the previous statutes had required the action "be in form, trespass, assault and battery, and false imprisonment..."[29] The pleading of such was *pro forma*. Edward Bates, Lincoln's Attorney General, later noted that Scott's suit was "an ordinary suit for freedom, very common in our jurisprudence," and

> *For convenience the form of the action usually is (and is in this case) trespass, alleging an assault and battery and false imprisonment, so as to enable the defendant (the master), if he choose, to make a direct issue upon the freedom or slavery of the plaintiff, which is the real point and object of the action, by pleading, in justification of the alleged trespass, that the plaintiff is a slave....*[30]

At this point the Scotts' attorney made his first mistake. He stipulated that Dred's case would be the lead one, with Harriet's to be decided in accord with it. Harriet actually had the stronger case. As noted above, her slaveholder, Major Talliaferro, wrote that he freed her, and had personally married the Scotts, when slaves were not allowed to marry. Since slave status was matrilinear (a child's status depended upon that of his or her mother), if Harriet was free then so were her two daughters. If the only thing in dispute was Dred's status, Irene Emerson might not have fought it, and certainly would not have twice fought it all the way to the state Supreme Court. In 1846, Dred was somewhere in his early to mid-50s, around the median age at death for adult males of the times.[31] But the argument that Talliaferro had freed Harriet was never made, here or in the Scott's later federal suit. Perhaps the attorneys were never informed of the point, or perhaps with a sure winner of a case he did not feel the need for a second theory.

At the trial, the Scotts' attorney made a second, more obvious, mistake. They called two witnesses to testify that the late *Dr. Emerson* had held Dred as a slave, but the one witness called to establish that *Irene Emerson* had also done so turned out to be testifying from hearsay. The summary of his testimony:

> *I did not hire the negroes myself, it was my wife who made the arrangements with Mrs. Emerson about them; I know nothing of*

the hiring but what I have been told by my wife; did nothing but pay the hiring money to Colonel Sanford [Irene's father]. I supposed that it was for Mrs. Emerson.[32]

His testimony was ruled hearsay, and without it the jury found for Mrs. Emerson. The Scotts had lost their freedom suit because they had not proven that anyone claimed they were slaves!

The Scotts moved for a new trial, which was granted. Mrs. Emerson's attorney appealed that to the state Supreme Court, which took two years to rule that there could no appeal from the granting of a new trial.

Then in 1848 and 1849 St. Louis experienced twin disasters. At the very end of 1848, an epidemic of the deadly water-borne disease cholera broke out; before it ended it would kill a tenth of the city's population. If that were not enough, in May 1849, a burning steamboat broke free of its moorings. As it drifted downstream it collided with and ignited twenty-three other ships. From there the fire spread to the city and destroyed the entire commercial district – together with many lawyers' offices.

The case was finally retried in January 1850; the Scotts were represented by new attorneys, who called the wife of the witness in the first trial, and established that the Scotts were hired out as Irene Emerson's slaves. The jury returned a verdict that the Scotts were free.

But their quest was not yet over. Mrs. Emerson's attorneys appealed to the Missouri Supreme Court.

The Missouri Supreme Court: the Scotts are still slaves

In that court, the action remained a freedom suit with few political overtones. Mrs. Emerson's attorney did not attack the Missouri Compromise – "Admitting, for the sake of argument, that Congress had the constitutional power to enact this section of the law, we maintain that it is entirely local in this provision, and by express reservation Missouri is exempted from its operation."[33] That is, the Missouri Compromise outlawed slavery in some areas, but made slavery legal in Missouri, thus it would not be violated by treating the Scotts as slaves once they returned to Missouri.

(This argument was a replay of a theme that had arisen in British law. In *Rex v. Knowles, ex parte Somersett*,[34] Lord Mansfield had ruled that bringing a slave into England resulted in legal emancipation, since slavery was so extraordinary a state that only legislation could authorize it. Slavery was "incapable of being introduced on any reasons, moral or political, but only by positive law [statute], which preserves its force long after the reasons, occasions, and time itself from whence it was created, is erased from memory." Half a century later, *The Slave Grace*[35] distinguished *Somersett*, finding that a slave thus freed in England would revert to slavery if they returned to the West Indies, British possessions that allowed slavery).

In the Missouri Supreme Court, Mrs. Emerson prevailed in a 2-1 decision. The majority overruled its long line of precedent in holding that the Scotts had reverted to slavery by their return; within Missouri, their status was that given by Missouri law, not by that of Illinois or the Wisconsin Territory. "It is a humiliating spectacle," the majority wrote, "to see the courts of a State confiscating the property of her own citizens by the command of a foreign law."[36] If the legal status created by those domains was to be recognized as binding in Missouri, it must be by interstate comity, which the court now rejected.

> *An attempt has been made to show that the comity extended to the laws of other States is a matter of discretion.... If it is a matter of discretion, that discretion must be controlled by circumstances. Times are not now as they were when the former decisions on this subject were made. Since they not only individuals but States have been possessed with a dark and fell spirit in relation to slavery, whose gratification is sought in the pursuit of measures, whose inevitable consequences must be the overthrow and destruction of our government. Under such circumstances it does not behoove the State of Missouri to show the least countenance to any measure which might gratify this spirit.*[37]

Judge Hamilton Gamble (later the wartime governor of Missouri) dissented; he argued first against the court departing from its 29 years of precedent, "I regard the question as conclusively settled, by repeated adjudications of this court, and if I doubted or denied the propriety of those decisions, I would not feel myself at more at liberty to overturn them than I would another other series of decisions, by which the law upon any other question was settled." Second, he pointed out that when an owner freed a slave in another state, and the act was challenged in Missouri (if, for example, the former owner died and his heirs argued the slave had not been legally freed and so was their property), Missouri asked whether the emancipation sufficed under the other state's laws; if it did, it was also binding in Missouri. The Illinois constitution provided that any slaves brought into the state would automatically be freed, so a slave owner who entered that state could not complain of that happening: "It is as much his voluntary act, as if he had executed a deed of emancipation." Judge Gamble's arguments were persuasive, but his one vote did not carry the day.

Irene Emerson had won, and it was a *major* victory for slavery in Missouri. Residence in a free state or territory had been the basis for most freedom prior to that point in time; it was so widely employed that slave deeds of sale often required the seller to warrant that the slaves had never resided on free land. Now that legal concept was entirely obliterated.

Irene Emerson probably learned of the ruling by letter. In 1849 or possibly 1850 she had moved to Massachusetts, to live with two of her sisters, who had relocated there. The date of the move is bounded by two events. On March 28, 1849, she sold a large parcel of St. Louis realty for $5,700.[38] And on November 21, 1850, she married Dr. Calvin Chaffee, in Springfield, Massachusetts.[39] We will hear more of Dr. Chaffee later.

Was Irene the Scotts' real opponent?

We are left to wonder at Irene's opposition to the Scotts' freedom suit, particularly its later stages. Irene had likely moved to Massachusetts before the second trial, and was certainly there during the second appeal. After her victory there, she appears to have ignored the Scotts; she didn't try to sell them, or hire them out. Why take so risky an appeal, using an argument that ran against nearly thirty years of precedent?

The legal costs of the battle were probably quite high. Her attorney, George W. Goode, a graduate of the University of Virginia, was one of the best in the city. He billed accordingly – in one land dispute that he took to the U.S. Supreme Court, he received a fee of $60,000, or over $1.7 million in modern money.[40]

So why did Irene fight out the freedom suit, and in particular take the second appeal? By 1852, whether the Scotts were free or slaves made no practical difference to her.

But there were other people in St. Louis who *did* have an interest in the question the appeal raised. Irene's brother John had married into the Chouteau family, the *very* wealthy and powerful family that descended from Auguste Chouteau, the cofounder of St. Louis.[41] The extent of their influence (and personal exploration) can be measured by the fact that there is a county named Chouteau in Montana, a city named Chouteau in Oklahoma, and that the capital of South Dakota is Pierre, named for Pierre Chouteau, Jr.

The Chouteau wealth and power initially lay in land – at one point they had owned the entire of St. Louis County – and fur trading. From there they had expanded into transportation, building railroads and plank roads, operating steamboats, and branched out into mining (one of their iron mines employed 2,000 men in its heyday).[42]

The Chouteaus had a personal interest in restricting freedom suits, since they had been on the receiving end of a good many of them. A list of such lawsuits shows that, by the time Dred and Harriet filed theirs, 214 such suits are known to have been filed, and 12 of those were against the Chouteaus, four them against Pierre Chouteau, Jr., the family patriarch.[43] Indeed, when the Scotts filed their freedom suit, Pierre had two freedom suit appeals pending in the Missouri Supreme Court.[44]

The Chouteau family had a strong interest in curtailing freedom suits, the money to back a legal fight, influence over Irene, and likely enough "insider knowledge" to know the Missouri Supreme Court was ready to overturn its precedent.

In an interview given a half-century after the event, Irene cited the Chouteaus as the reason the case stayed alive. A *New York Times* reporter summed up her side of the matter:

[T]he case would probably have been compromised in some manner if it had not been for a peculiar occurrence, which happened to take place just before the suit was brought. This was the wholesale flight of all the negroes belonging to the Chouteau family into which John Sandford [Irene's brother] had married. In all, seventeen escaped in one night, and got over into Illinois, and from there into Canada, and the family was so angry over the matter that its members persuaded Sandford to fight out the case to the last. Accordingly, Sandford took up the matter on his own account and carried it on, Mrs. Chaffee [Irene] not knowing much about it.... [45]

Some of this may be obfuscation: decades after the event, Irene had reason to minimize her own role. The connection between the slaves' escape and resisting the Scotts' freedom suit is tenuous; perhaps that was just the excuse the Chouteaus gave Irene. But that the Chouteaus had an interest in curtailing freedom suits, and had the ability to finance such an effort, is beyond question. Note that the claim was that "John Sandford" was the man the Chouteaus persuaded to "fight the case to the last." We will hear more of Mr. "Sandford," and the reference suggests that the Chouteaus' backing did not stop with the Missouri Supreme Court decision.

Whoever was behind the case, the Scotts' quest for freedom seemed to have ended with the Missouri Supreme Court's decision. Then their search took another turn.

IV

The Scotts Turn to Federal Court, suing John F. A. Sanford

If the Scotts' quest for freedom had ended at this point, they would at best be a tiny and obscure footnote in American legal history. Who today knows that Missouri once had "freedom suits," let alone that an 1852 decision blocked most of them?

Initially, the Scott's cause did seem destined for such an end. Their state freedom suit sat in limbo for over a year, as the trial judge to whom their state case had been remanded still declined to enter judgment in Irene's favor.

Then something happened. We will probably never know what it was.

What we do know is this: pursuant to the Missouri court's orders, the sheriff had "hired out" Dred Scott to attorney Charles Edmund LeBeaume, who was one of the Blow family's in-laws.[46] LeBeaume in turn brought the Scotts' case to the attention of another attorney, Roswell Field.

Field was an interesting fellow, born and raised in Vermont, he moved to St. Louis in 1839. He was reputed an excellent practitioner of realty law, a complicated and profitable legal field in the new state. Louisiana land titles began with a land grant from a monarch, and the state had been part of France from its settlement, and part of Spain after 1763, then again part of France from 1800 until its 1803 sale to the United States. Field was fluent in English, French, and Spanish, which gave him a significant advantage in interpreting and arguing the meaning of the land grants, and of later deeds and marriage settlements. There is, however, no indication that he had a comparable advantage in the field of constitutional law or, indeed, any experience there at all. This may explain some of the decisions he made and the course that the federal case followed.

Field felt that the Scotts could take a second try at freedom by filing suit in federal district court, under what is known as diversity jurisdiction. The Constitution gave federal courts limited jurisdiction: they can't accept just any suit, it must fall into one of several classifications. Two were significant for private litigants: federal question and diversity. Today federal question jurisdiction, where a federal court settles matters of federal law, is by far the more important. But in the 1850s, there were few federal laws on which a private lawsuit could be based. Federal courts still operated under the Judiciary Act of 1789, which gave them very limited federal question jurisdiction,[47] leaving diversity jurisdiction as their main civil business.

Diversity jurisdiction arose out of the Founding Fathers' concern that a citizen of one state, sued in another state, might find local courts (whose judges were often elected) biased against him. Their solution was to allow suits between citizens of different states to be brought in federal court, where the judge at least came into office due to federal rather than state patronage, and held a lifetime appointment.

(We return again to the concept of an alternate reality. Today federal courts are a major part of the American judicial system. In the 1850s, they were not. The federal court for the District of Louisiana held its sessions by borrowing courtrooms from the St. Louis courts. When those were occupied – as they were on the day of the Dred Scott trial – it held court in any room that it could find or rent. The Dred Scott case was tried in "a small back room over a Main Street store.").[48] The judge was Robert W. Wells, who had previously served as Attorney General of the state.

Then and now, a federal lawsuit begins with a complaint (then referred to as a declaration) which sets out the basis of the plaintiff's claims. The first sentence of Dred Scott's complaint claimed diversity jurisdiction: "Dred Scott of St. Louis in the State of Missouri and a citizen of the State of Missouri, complains of John F. A. Sandford of the City of New York and a citizen of the State of New York...." The complaint asserted that "Sandford" (his actual name, as we shall see, was Sanford) had, in January 1853, assaulted and falsely imprisoned Scott, leaving him in such fear that he "could not attend to his business & thereby lost great gains & profits which he might have made & otherwise would have made..." Dred sought damages of $2,500.

A second count alleged the same had been done to Harriet, and a third count alleged it had been done to their daughters, with the result that Dred lost the "comfort, society, and assistance" of his family members.[49] As with the earlier state suit, this does not mean that Sanford was a brawler; these were standard "boilerplate" claims meant to test the issue of Scott's slavery. It was a civil claim for assault and false imprisonment, silently raising the slavery issue – if Scott was a slave, John F. A. Sanford had the legal right to strike and imprison him, if Scott was free, Sanford was legally in the wrong. It is noteworthy that at this stage the entire focus was upon Dred's situation; the situation of Harriet and the children (who, as noted above, had the stronger cases) were invoked only as contributions to the damages Dred claimed from John F. A. Sanford, the man who was holding Dred's family as slaves.

But at this point one question becomes glaringly obvious....

V
Who in the Devil Is John F. A. "Sandford"????

Let's stop for a bit of historical review. In 1833, Dred Scott becomes Dr. Emerson's slave. In 1844, Emerson died, and Scott passed to Irene Emerson. From 1846 until 1852, Scott sues Irene Emerson in state court, ending with the Missouri Supreme Court ruling that the Scott family were *Irene Emerson's* slaves.

Then, in 1853, Scott instead sues someone named John F. A. Sandford, alleging that Sandford holds him in slavery, *and Sanford agrees to that claim*. In fact, the two sides agree that Sandford acquired the Scott family from Dr. Emerson while Dr. Emerson lived, meaning that Irene never had any claim to the family at all.

Something very strange is going on here....

Who was John F. A. Sanford?

We actually know more about John F. A. Sanford (that the Supreme Court misspelled his name as "Sandford" indicates how nominal was his involvement in the case) than we do about most participants in the Scott case. He was born in Virginia, and in July 1821, at age 15 or 16, he was admitted to the U.S. Military Academy at West Point, from which he resigned seven months later.[50] (He was later often identified as "Major," but it was presumably a militia rank).

Thereafter, he went west and became a frontiersman. At age 19, he put his name as a witness to treaties with the Kansa tribe in 1825, and with the Sauk and Fox in 1830 and 1837.[51] He became sub-agent to an Indian Agent, in which role he was responsible for the upper Missouri, and lived two years among the Mandans. In 1831 he took a group of four Indians to Washington DC, and on his return escorted the painter George Catlin, who became famous for his Indian portraits.[52]

At that point, the frontiersman's life took an unusual turn. He must have been a good deal more polished than the typical mountain man, since in 1831 he married Emile Chouteau, daughter of Pierre Chouteau, Jr., head of the powerful Chouteau family (which, as we have seen, had a major interest in curtailing slave freedom suits).

In 1833 Sanford resigned as sub-agent to become an employee of Pierre Chouteau, Jr, and rapidly rose. He became Chouteau's right-hand man and eventually his business partner. He served as his father-in-law's Washington lobbyist (lobbying, and in particular ensuring that Indian treaties would pay the Indian trappers' debts to the fur company, was a major concern). When in 1841 Chouteau opened a New York office – which became the critical one for maintaining trading links with European fur buyers – Sanford headed it.[53]

He was also a founding director of the Illinois Central Railroad Company, an enormous economic and technical operation,[54] and partner in Pierre Chouteau Jr., Sanford & Co., which imported railway rails.[55] He is reported to have been a commercial banker as well, and to have been worth three million dollars, the equivalent of over ninety million today.[56]

Sanford's nephew would later describe his uncle's business empire:

He was then the active partner, in the firm of P. Chouteau, Jr., Sanford and Company, doing a general banking business in New York, mainly connected with railroad construction. They had recently been instrumental in the building of the Illinois Central, and my uncle was a director and a prime mover in that enterprise. He, in association with Alsop & Chauncey, Edward Learned, Charles Gould, David Leavitt, Mr. Manice and others, had taken over the contract of Page and Bacon, bankrupt contractors, for building the Ohio and Mississippi Railroad, and had made a contract for his firm to furnish the iron rails to be imported from England, to complete the railroad.[57]

Sanford's work was both lucrative and time-consuming: an 1857 newspaper article refers to the "herculean mental labors demanded by the gigantic interests entrusted to him," his "brilliant success," and "[t]he tide of wealth that flowed upon him."[58]

Lobbyist, railroad director, banker, millionaire – yes, John F. A. Sanford was not the typical frontiersman!

Which bring us to the question: why would such a person have been interested in buying an elderly slave in St. Louis, whose services the sheriff was renting out for $5 a month?

Yet the Dred Scott case was tried upon an "agreed statement of facts" – that is, no witnesses need be called since both parties agreed these were the facts – which recited:

> *Before the commencement of this suit, said Dr. Emerson sold and conveyed the plaintiff,* [Dred Scott] *said Harriet, Eliza, and Lizzie, to the defendant* [John F. A. Sanford], *as slaves, and the defendant has ever since claimed to hold them and each of them as slaves.*[59]

The agreed statement of facts has one problem: it cannot possibly be true.

Dr. Emerson sold the Scott family to Sanford? Emerson died over a decade earlier, in 1844. Thereafter, all the evidence is that *Irene* Emerson claimed the Scotts. In the Scotts' state freedom suit she was named as the slaveowner, she agreed to that claim, the testimony was that she "hired out" their services, she appealed to the Missouri Supreme Court, and that court ruled that she owned the Scotts. But in the Scotts' federal suit John F. A. Sanford's name appears out of nowhere, as the fellow who owns and had long owned the Scott family.

Why would the Scotts sue Sanford?

So why did Scott's attorney sue Sanford? After their case reached the Supreme Court, Scott's attorney, Roswell Field, gave this explanation, to a Supreme Court attorney he hoped to interest in the case:

> *Several years ago Dred brought a suit for his freedom against Mrs. Emerson, the widow of his former master in the state court... the Supreme Court (Gamble dissenting) overruled all its prior decisions & reversed the judgment, remanding the case for another trial. See the case reported 15 Mo Rep 576.*

> *At this stage of the case I was applied to by C. E. Lebeaume Esq for advice. As Dred in the meantime had been sold with his family to Sanford of New York who was accustomed to visit Missouri, I advised the institution of a suit in the Circuit Court of the United States....*[60]

This chronology puts the sale of the Scotts to Sanford as sometime after the March, 1852, Missouri ruling.

But the agreed statement of facts said that *Dr. Emerson* had sold the Scotts to Sanford. How could Dr. Emerson have made that sale, when he had died eight years before?

The historians search in vain for the answer

Historians have long puzzled over Sanford's sudden appearance as the defendant. Some speculate that he might have been sued as the executor of Dr. Emerson's will. But while Sanford *was* mentioned in the will, as one of two executors, he failed to qualify under Iowa law, and the other person named, George L. Davenport, served as sole executor.[61]

One oft-repeated explanation of John Sanford's involvement is that, after Irene moved to Massachusetts in 1849-50, Sanford was left to manage her affairs in St. Louis, and was thus sued as her agent *de facto*.[62] But there is no reason to believe that Irene even *had* any assets in St. Louis to administer. Dr. Emerson's St. Louis probate estate was limited to a parcel of realty and some furniture.[63] Irene sold the realty in 1849, before moving to Massachusetts,[64] and presumably sold the furniture or took it with her. Further, if she did have assets in St. Louis, why would she have asked Sanford, living in New York City, to manage them?

And why do both these explanations clash with the agreed statement of facts, which claims Dr. Emerson sold the Scotts to Sanford?

The most encyclopedic treatment of Dred Scott, Don E. Fehrenbacher's 741-page, Pulitzer Prize winning, *The Dred Scott Case*, despairs of determining how John F. A. Sanford came to be the defendant:

> *Thus the odor of conspiracy detected in Dred Scott v. Sandford proves to be extremely elusive, and certain puzzling things about its origin do not add up to a "fabricated case." Unless more positive documentary evidence is discovered, the suspicion of a political plot should probably be put aside.*[65]

"Unless more positive documentary evidence is discovered..."

The Mystery Resolved: Meet Rep. Calvin Chaffee

There is a simple explanation for why Dred Scott's attorney sued John F. A. Sanford.

First, understand that Sanford was the brother of Irene Emerson (maiden name Eliza Irene Sanford), whom Scott had sued in his state freedom suit, and whom the Missouri Supreme Court had ruled was his family's owner.

Second, make the acquaintance of Irene's second husband, and thus John Sanford's brother in law, Dr. Calvin Chaffee.

Chaffee was a Springfield, Massachusetts physician. He was elected to the U.S. House of Representatives in 1854 as a member of the American (or "Know Nothing")[66] Party and re-elected in 1856 as a Republican.

The *Boston Herald* described him as "a sturdy representative of the Massachusetts anti-slavery sentiment during his two terms of service in Congress."[67] His hometown *Springfield Republican* commented on his "courage and decision in sustaining the anti-slavery sentiment of

Massachusetts at its full force," while warding off "his share of threats of violence."[68] It related one incident, occurring after the famous assault by Rep. Preston Brooks, who had severely beaten Sen. Charles Sumner with a cane on the Senate floor. Brooks, drunk, told Chaffee "I thrashed one Massachusetts man today, and I'd like to thrash another."

Chaffee responded by buying a revolver, the story continued, adding that Rep. Aiken of South Carolina saw Chaffee slide the revolver out of his pocket and into his desk on the House floor. Startled, Aiken asked if Chaffee was ready to use it and Chaffee responded, "If any of your chivalry irritate me, I shall certainly use this revolver." The *Republican* story concluded: "After that, Dr. Chaffee's southern friends were not only civil but cordial."

Rep. Calvin Chaffee was, in short, not one of the leaders of the Congressional anti-slavery movement, but certainly one of its more dedicated foot soldiers, down to the point of being prepared to shoot it out on the House floor!

The conclusion is obvious: John F. A. Sanford agreed to be named in Dred Scott's lawsuit as a stand-in, to keep his sister's (and her husband's) names out of it. It would not do for a prominent anti-slavery Congressman to be named as defendant in a slave's suit for his freedom, in a case destined for the Supreme Court!

But that case does not rest on circumstantial evidence alone: we have the testimony of an eyewitness.

A half century after John F. A. Sanford's death, his nephew, John Sanford Barnes, wrote his own autobiography, a fascinating piece of writing, now lodged in the New York Historical Society library.[69] During the Civil War, Barnes was a lieutenant commander in the Union navy, in which capacity he met Abraham Lincoln, Mrs. Lincoln, General Grant, General Sherman, and other great figures of the age. (Curiously enough, as a boy he met Dr. Calvin Chaffee, who sewed up his dog's injuries).[70]

In his work, Barnes describes his uncle's and aunt's roles in Dred Scott (bear in mind that parts of this are hearsay from Irene, who would have had an incentive to downplay her involvement in the case):

Of course it was embarrassing to Dr. Chaffee, to have his wife appear as a slave owner, opposing his claim to freedom, so Dred was nominally transferred to her brother, my uncle, John F. A. Sanford.... Living with my uncle during this time, I naturally took a great interest in the case, and heard him express his views and was present on several occasions when the Honorable Reverdy Johnson [the attorney who would represent the pro-slavery side in *Dred Scott*] *was his guest at dinner. The object I have in making these allusions to the Dred Scott case is mainly to give a little of the inside history not known and never published, and which may interest our family, if no one else. My Aunt Irene, then Mrs. Chaffee, had distinctly refused to have any hand or part in the suit, and she also had declined to sell him, or exercise any right of property in Dred Scott, who, so far as her legal ownership was concerned, had been absolutely free ever since the death of her husband, Dr. Emmerson* [sic]. *She had only a life interest in him, the reversion being in her daughter, a minor, and for whom her brother John, was the nominal Trustee. She had particularly, since her second marriage to Dr. Chaffee, earnestly desired that Dred and his family should be manumitted wholly and legally, but was advised that this could not be legally accomplished by any act of hers.*

Except in his quality as Trustee for his minor niece Henrietta Emmerson, my uncle was not at any time his owner, and was improperly named as the individual defendant. This and other matters connected therewith were discussed in my hearing between Mr. Johnson and my uncle, and as I remember, my uncle, himself a slave owner, relegated the question to the care of Mr. Johnson and his colleagues most emphatically, moreover disavowing any personal interest, and only consenting to continuance of the case in his name, on the argument that it was his public and patriotic duty to aid in quieting a discussion injurious to the country's welfare. From the first he had refused to bear any part of the expense for lawyer's fees or incidental expenses, and always desired that his sister and himself should be cleared of any further litigation that did not involve the payment of damages by the legal owner of the worthless negro. Who retained Mr. Johnson and Senator Geyer, his attorneys of record, or who paid them their fees or expenses I don't know, if they were ever paid, but I do know that neither mu uncle nor my aunt ever paid them a penny, nor was ever

*any demand made upon them. More than once Mr. Johnson said:
"Now, Sanford, there will be no charge whatever to you or Mrs.
Chaffee on this account; the expenses will be provided elsewhere".
And it was upon this expressed condition that the suit went forward
to its ultimate decision, in which of course, my uncle whose birth,
antecedents and his entire sympathy with the Southern view, was
in full accord, while my aunt, influenced by her husband, Dr.
Chaffee - a pronounced free soil member of congress - was wholly
opposed to being considered as having any personal interest in
Dred, or in the question involved in the suit.[71]*

John F. A. Sanford was simply a stand-in, a "straw man" to hide
the real parties in interest. The agreed statement of facts was falsified,
down to the statement that *Dr. Emerson* had transferred the Scotts to
Sanford; the only logical reason for that statement was to keep Irene's
name completely out of the case.

This could not have been a secret to any of the attorneys involved.
Reverdy Johnson, Sanford's attorney, had set the arrangement up.
Scott's attorney, Roswell Field, drafted the complaint that named
Sanford as the defendant who was holding the Scotts in slavery.

There is further evidence of pre-arrangement in the timing of the
lawsuit. A critical second step in any lawsuit involves having the
summons (which orders the defendant to appear) and complaint
served upon the defendant. The Judiciary Act of 1789 did not allow
service outside the federal district in which the suit was filed; to sue
someone in the District of Missouri, you must serve them in the
District of Missouri, and John F. A. Sanford was a very busy New
York City businessman. But the lawsuit was filed on November 2,
1853, and on that same day the U.S. Marshal located Sanford in St.
Louis and served him with the summons and complaint![72]

It is doubtful that Sanford spent a lot of time in St. Louis. Even
with the new railroads, travel between New York City and St. Louis
was not a simple matter. When, seven years later, Lincoln made the
railroad journey from Springfield, Illinois to New York City, the
round-trip took five full days and nights, with five changes of train
each way.[73] New York to St. Louis could have been no easier: St.
Louis was the next stop after Springfield on that line, about ninety
miles to its south.

One other thing is noteworthy here. According to John Sanford

Barnes' account, the attorney who convinced his uncle to become the defendant in the lawsuit was Reverdy Johnson. Reverdy Johnson was not a St. Louis lawyer; he was a Marylander, a former Attorney General of the United States, and *very* pro-slavery. At this point in life he had acquired a specialty.

Arguing cases before the United States Supreme Court.

it at length; discussions ensued and some excitement prevailed all over the country.

Living with my uncle during this time, I naturally took a great interest in the case, and heard him express his views and was present on several occasions when the Honorable Reverdy Johnson was his guest at dinner. The object I have in making these allusions to the Dred Scott case, is mainly to give a little of the inside history not known and never published, and which may interest our family, if no one else. My Aunt Irene, then Mrs. Chaffee, had distinctly refused to have any hand or part in the suit, and she also had declined to sell him, or exercise any right of property in Dred Scott, who so far as her legal ownership was concerned had been absolutely free, ever since the death of her husband, Dr. Emmerson. She had only a life interest in him, the reversion being in her daughter, a minor, and for whom her brother John, was the nominal Trustee. She had particularly, since her second marriage to Dr. Chaffee, earnestly desired that Dred and his family should be manumitted wholly and legally, but was advised that this could not be legally accomplished by any act of hers.

Except in his quality as Trustee for his minor niece, Henrietta Emmerson, my uncle was not at any time his owner, and was improperly named as the individual defendant. This and other matters connected therewith were discussed in my hearing between Mr. Johnson and my uncle, and as I remember, my uncle himself a slave owner, relegated the question to the care of Mr. Johnson and his colleagues most emphatically, moreover disavowing any personal interest, and only consenting to continuance of the case in

The Egotistigraphy of John Sanford Barnes (*ca.* 1910) (New-York Historical Society, Naval Collection).

his name, on the argument thatiit was his public and patriotic
duty to aid in quieting a discussion injurious to the country's
welfare.   From the first he had refused to bear any part of the
expense for lawyer's fees or incidental expenses, and always desired that his sister and himself should be cleared of any further litigation that did not involve the payment of damages by
the legal owner of the worthless negro.   Who retained Mr.
Johnson and Senator Geyer, his attorneys of record, or who paid
them their fees and expenses I don't know, if they were ever paid,
but I do know that neither my uncle nor my aunt ever paid them a
penny, nor was ever any demand made upon them.   More than once
Mr. Johnson said: "Now, Sanford, there will be no charge whatever
to you or Mrs. Chaffee on this account; the expenses will be provided elsewhere."   And it was upon this expressed condition that
the suit went forward to its ultimate decision, in which of course,
my uncle, whose birth, antecedents and his entire sympathy with
the Southern view, was in full accord, while my aunt, influenced
by her husband, Dr. Chaffee, a pronounced free soil member of Congress
was wholly opposed to being considered as having any personal
interest in Dred, or in the question involved in the suit.   The
final decision, declaring all slavery restrictions unconstitutional, aroused a storm of indignation, and roused the free states to
the point of fury.   Judge Taney's announcement that a negro has
no rights which a white man was bound to respect, focussed public
wrath upon him, while the entire South burst out in frantic applause.

VI
The Path to the Supreme Court

It is easy to see why the pro-slavery Reverdy Johnson would want to take a slavery case to the Supreme Court. The Court's membership was then split 5 - 4 in favor of Justices from slave States,[74] and the four from free States had so far "distinguished themselves by defending national power to recapture fugitive slaves."[75] Chief Justice Taney was *very* pro-slavery; moreover, he had as Attorney General ruled that free blacks were not citizens, which would become an issue in the case.[76] Three of the Justices owned slaves, and two more were former slaveowners.[77] The Court had recently handed down *Strader v. Graham*,[78] ruling in favor of a slaveowner on arguments quite similar to those raised in Scott's appeal.

Johnson was, in short, looking at a sure win.

It is harder to see why Roswell Field, Dred Scott's attorney, would agree to such a course. Obviously, he had to agree. He had to file the lawsuit naming John F. A. Sanford and, after he lost, take the appeal, along the way signing onto the agreed statement of facts with its clearly false claim that Dr. Emerson had sold the Scotts to Sanford.

It is also obvious that Field knew the federal case he was filing was destined for the Supreme Court. The Scotts' state freedom suit was still pending in the St. Louis court when the federal case was filed (the Missouri Supreme Court had remanded the case to the trial court but that court had never entered a final judgment). After Scott's federal suit was filed, both sides agreed to delay the state suit until the Supreme Court could settle the matter. The St. Louis trial court files show an entry: "Continued by consent, (awaiting decision of Supreme Court of the United States.)."[79] That this case would reach the Supreme Court was intent, not speculation.

What could Roswell Field have been thinking? He seems to have been the type of attorney that appellate attorneys dread: an idealist. A fellow who believes that if an impartial view of the law favors his side, he must inevitably win. When Dred's case was pending in the Supreme Court, he wrote a letter to the attorney handling the appeal:

I rec'd your brief in the Dred Scott case and your two letters relating to it. I have delayed writing to you in the expectation that the case would soon be decided & that I should have the opportunity of congratulating you on the result.... I entirely concur with you in the opinion that there could be no doubt at all about the issue if factious politicks did not mingle in the counsels of the court.[80]

They would win if factions and politics did not interfere? In 1856, the slavery issue was *all about* factions and politics!

We also know that Field could be a very stubborn man when he thought he was in the right. In 1832, when he was practicing law in Vermont, he fell in love with 18-year old Mary Almira Phelps, who happened to be engaged to someone else.[81] He and Phelps married secretly, after which she returned to her family. Two weeks later, she wrote Field that she loved her former fiancé and asked Field to destroy the marriage certificate.

Instead of tearing up the certificate and being thankful for having escaped a lifetime commitment to someone so fickle, and in any event who now loved someone else, Field embarked on a nine-year series of legal battles that included three trips to the Vermont Supreme Court (which finally ruled the marriage invalid), seeking the intervention of grand juries in two states, an indictment of her brother, and a lawsuit against her mother.[82]

Was Dred's attorney tricked into a doomed Supreme Court fight?

Field seems to have seen the Scott's case as raising a narrow issue with a limited risk and a potential for great gains. *Dred Scott*'s most stunning blow was its holding that the Missouri Compromise was unconstitutional because Congress had no power to restrict slavery in the territories. But this issue did not clearly arise until the case's first oral argument in the Supreme Court.[83] Field had written his Supreme Court cocounsel that the case raised a single issue: "The question involved is the much vexed one whether the removal by the master of his slave to Illinois or Wisconsin works an absolute emancipation of the slave."[84] That is, whether the slave is *absolutely* emancipated, so that he remains free if he returns to a slave state.

If this was the only issue, the anti-slavery side risked little by proceeding. If the Court sided with the Missouri Supreme Court on this issue, it would mean that a slave taken to free territory became a slave again upon returning to a slave State – which was already the legal status quo in Missouri and many other slave states.[85]

This in turn suggests that Field was suckered by the opposing attorneys. Recall that Sanford's nephew, who was at the dinner table when Sanford agreed to pose as defendant, said his uncle "agreed on the argument that it was his public and patriotic duty to aid in quieting a discussion injurious to the country's welfare." The issue of Congressional power over slavery in the territories fits that description, better than does the narrow question of the status of a former slave who returns to a slave state. *If this interpretation of Sanford's words is correct, then Reverdy Johnson was planning to attack such Congressional power, and the Missouri Compromise, even before Dred Scott's federal lawsuit was initiated.*

The Scott's federal suit in the trial court

Field filed his action, and Sanford's St. Louis attorneys wasted no time raising the issues of slavery and the citizenship of free blacks. They began by objecting to the trial court's jurisdiction, via what was termed a "plea in abatement," though they titled it "Plea to the Jurisdiction of the Court."[86] Diversity jurisdiction required that the parties on either side be citizens, not just residents, of different states, and, Sanford's attorneys argued,

> the said plaintiff Dred Scott is not a citizen of the State of Missouri as alleged in his declaration – because he is a negro of African descent – his ancestors were of pure African blood and were brought into this country and sold as negro slaves – and of this the said Sanford is ready to testify. Wherefore he prays judgment whether this court can or will take further cognizance of the action aforesaid.

Judge Welles ruled that the court did have jurisdiction, because Dred was either a Missouri citizen or sufficiently like a citizen (in that he resided in Missouri and, if he was free, had the capacity to own property there) to qualify. In this Welles followed the approach used by the Supreme Court to hold that corporations – artificial, non-human legal entities – were *sufficiently like* a citizen to qualify for diversity jurisdiction.[87]

Sanford's attorneys then filed a "Plea of Defendant," to answer Dred Scott's complaint. It squarely raised the slavery issue:

And for a further plea in his behalf as to the making of the said assault upon the same Dred Scott ... and imprisoning him, and keeping and detaining him in prison ... the said Dred Scott was a negro slave, the lawful property of the defendant, and as such he gently laid his hands upon him and only restrained him of such liberty as he had a right to do.[88]

The case came up for trial in May 1854. No witnesses were called, the parties having submitted the agreed statement of facts. Both sides moved for a "directed verdict" – a jury instruction that the facts and law were so clear that the jury *must* rule for their side. The trial court turned down Scott's motion, but granted that of Sanford: "The jury are instructed that, upon the facts in this case, the law is with the defendant."[89] The jury accordingly returned a verdict in Sanford's favor, ruling that "the plaintiff is a negro slave and the property of defendant."[90] From that ruling Field appealed Dred Scott's case to the Supreme Court.[91]

At that point, Field had a problem. Even more so than today, Supreme Court practice was a specialized field of law. It required an attorney to be in or near Washington, D.C. And, unlike today, very little was done in writing, and the case was presented by oral argument, which often spanned days. Thus, a Supreme Court attorney had to have a powerful voice, rhetorical skills, and the ability to speak for days at a time. Field had no such attorney on his side.

His search for one began a week before the trial (yet another sign that the case was seen as destined for the Supreme Court) when an article about the case in a St. Louis newspaper ended: "Dred is, of course, poor and without any powerful friends. But no doubt he will find at the bar of the Supreme Court some able and generous advocate, who will do all he can to establish his right to be free."[92] This was followed by a pamphlet that ended with a similar appeal.[93] But no volunteers stepped forward.

The Scotts' case comes before the Supreme Court

Eventually, Field wrote to Montgomery Blair, a Maryland attorney and Washington insider. Blair was a logical choice: a Missouri free-soil advocate, he had recently moved to the Maryland suburbs of Washington, where he practiced before the Supreme Court (although his critics insisted that his voice was too high-pitched and he lacked the proper rhetorical flourishes). By the time *Dred Scott* was brought to Blair's attention, the Supreme Court had already accepted the appeal. Blair' choices were down to letting Scott's case fail by default, or tackling it himself. He chose the latter.

Whoever was handling the case for John F. A. Sanford fielded two first-rate advocates to argue Sanford's side. The first was, of course, Reverdy Johnson, who had persuaded Sanford to pose as the defendant. A former Senator and Attorney General, Johnson was certainly one of the top Supreme Court practitioners and "considered the foremost constitutional lawyer in the nation."[94] He had been arguing Supreme Court cases since 1827, when he had argued alongside his co-counsel, Roger Taney, who now sat as Chief Justice.[95] Sanford's other advocate was Senator Henry S. Geyer, who had been considered a leader of the St. Louis bar prior to his election.

Today, the Supreme Court usually rations oral argument at a half-hour per side; it was otherwise in the 1850s. The first argument in Dred Scott began on February 10, 1856, and spanned six days. The arguments had one surprise: Blair had assumed the main issues were Scott's ability to sue in diversity jurisdiction, that is, whether he was a citizen of Missouri, and whether upon his return to Missouri his status returned to that of a slave. But Johnson and Geyer ducked the second issue. Instead they argued that Scott has never been free in the first place. Congress had no constitutional power to restrict slavery in the territories, meaning that the Missouri Compromise was unconstitutional and slavery had been legal in the Wisconsin Territory when Dr. Emerson took the Scotts to Fort Snelling.

By the close of the first argument in the case, Blair knew that the anti-slavery cause faced real risks. The issue of Congressional power to restrict slavery had been prominently raised – a printed (and doubtless condensed) version of Blair's presentation at the second argument devotes 14 pages to the subject.[96]

Whatever hopes Blair could have had would have faded when newspaper "leaks" began reporting that he would lose 7-2.[97] Blair wrote former president Martin van Buren: "It seems to be the impressions that the opinion of the Court will be adverse to my client & to the power of Congress over the territories."[98]

The Supreme Court held several conferences (private meetings at which the Justices debated and took votes on cases). The interjection of a new constitutional question, the Missouri Compromise and Congress's power over slavery in the territories, probably determined the result: the Court ordered a second series of arguments for December 1856.

This time, Montgomery Blair found a co-counsel. George Ticknor Curtis, a Massachusetts anti-slavery activist, came on to assist him with the constitutional question. (He was also the brother of Justice Curtis; in those days there was little concern about conflicts of interest). For four days, Blair and Curtis debated Johnson and Geyer in the crowded courtroom.

President Buchanan secretly lobbies Supreme Court Justices

The Court retired to consider its decision. Its multiple conferences suggested sharp divisions among the justices. What we know about those conferences is a result of some extraordinary, and quite irregular, correspondence between president-elect James Buchanan and members of the Court.

The election of 1856 had been an unusual one – the only one in which a major party refused to re-nominate its incumbent president, yet still won the election. Democratic incumbent Millard Fillmore lost his fight for re-nomination, and ran as a candidate of the American Party, getting 20% of the popular vote. The Democratic candidate, James Buchanan, got 45% of the popular vote and 174 electoral votes, while his Republican opponent, John C. Fremont, got 33% of the popular vote and 114 electoral votes.

Buchanan's inauguration was set for March 4, 1857. Before Buchanan's inaugural speech, Chief Justice Taney was observed to whisper something in the incoming president's ear. The pro-slavery Buchanan then delivered an address that said of the Dred Scott case that "it is a judicial question, which legitimately belongs to the Supreme Court of the United States, before whom it is now pending, and will, it is understood, be speedily and finally settled. To their decision, in common with all good citizens, I shall cheerfully submit..."[99]

Senator William Seward was, until Lincoln's sudden rise in 1860, the natural leader of the antislavery movement. Speaking on the Senate floor, he alleged that Taney had whispered a tip to Buchanan about the case's outcome:

The day of inauguration came – the first one among all the celebrations of that great national pageant that was to be desecrated by a coalition between the executive and judicial departments to undermine the National Legislature and the liberties of the people. The President, attended by the usual lengthened procession, arrived and took his seat on the portico. The Supreme Court attended him there, in robes which yet exacted public reverence. The people, unaware of the import of the whisperings carried on between the President and the Chief Justice, and imbued with veneration for both, filled the avenues and gardens as far away as the eye could reach.[100]

The next day, Seward charged, the Justices, "without even exchanging their silken robes for courtiers' gowns, paid their salutations to the President," and the day after that they announced their ruling in *Dred Scott*.

Chief Justice Taney was enraged at Seward's accusation, so angry that he told a friend he that, had Seward instead of Lincoln won the election of 1860, he would have refused to give Seward the oath of office.[101]

Taney's resentment may cloak feelings of guilt. Seward's "conspiracy theory" actually understated the case. Buchanan did not have to depend upon a few whispered words. *Two Supreme Court Justices had tipped the president off as to the Court's deliberations, the vote count, and even advised him on what he might want to say about the case in his inaugural address. While Taney was not one of them, he knew of and approved their effort. President Buchanan, in turn, had secretly lobbied a pivotal Justice to vote to strike down the Missouri Compromise.*

Washington was then a small town, and the ruling elite a tiny club that kept its secrets well. The secret correspondence was not revealed until long after the principals were dead, and even today we have only the Justices' letters to Buchanan, not his letters to them.[102]

In early February 1857, Buchanan wrote to his close friend Justice Catron. The subject was rather innocuous – was the Court going to rule before or after Buchanan's inauguration? Catron replied that that was up to the Chief Justice, but he would find out.

On February 10, Catron sent the president-elect a long letter headed "CONFIDENTIAL," and which was *not* innocuous. Justice Catron began by revealing the Court's deliberations at length.

Some of the judges will touch the question of power [over the territories], *others may, but that it will settle nothing, is my present opinion, no opinion can be expected to be announced before the end of month.*

On the contested question, my opinion is that Congress has power to govern the Territories by the fourth and third section of the constitution.... To hold that no power existed to govern Territories after a practice of 68 years would shock all the substantial lawyers of the country, and subject the court to the ridicule that the Nicholson letter received. Of course the securities contained in the Constitution limit the power....[103]

Catron went on to give his opinion that the treaty by which France sold the Louisiana Territory to the United States provided that the inhabitants of the land sold would be protected "in the free enjoyment of their liberty, property, and religion," To his mind, the reference to property (*i.e.* slaves) might settle the issue. Catron ended with "It is

47

11 o'clock and I must go to Court."

Nine days later, Catron penned a shorter, but even more improper, letter advising Buchanan what he may "safely" say about *Dred Scott* in his inaugural address. Catron advised saying that a constitutional challenge to the Missouri Compromise was pending in the Supreme Court, whose "high and independent character" would enable it to settle the issue, and that as president Buchanan would make no further comment on the matter. Catron added that "A majority of my Brethren will be forced up to this point by two dissentients." Reading that, Buchanan would have known that a majority of the Court was going to strike down the Missouri Compromise, with two dissents.

Catron went further, though, asking Buchanan to lobby Justice Grier, who, like Buchanan, was a Pennsylvanian and a Democrat. Grier, Catron wrote, was preparing an opinion that did not reach the Missouri Compromise issue. Grier's joining the majority position on that would be important, since then it could not be said that all the votes to strike the Compromise came from slave-state Justices.[104]

Will you drop Grier a line, saying how necessary it is - & how good the opportunity is, to settle the agitation by an affirmative decision of the Supreme Court, one way or the other. He ought not to occupy so doubtful a ground as the outside issue – that admitting the constitutionality of the Mo. Comp. line of 1820, still no domicile was acquired by the negro at Ft. Snelling & he returned to Missouri, he was not free. He has no doubt about the question on the main contest, but has been persuaded to take the smooth handle for the sake of repose.

Buchanan apparently (no copy survives) did as Catron asked. Thanks to Catron's advice, he knew that Grier was going to vote with the majority on the key issue – is Dred Scott still a slave? It only remained to convince him to join the part of Taney's opinion that would, as one ground for that conclusion, rule the Missouri Compromise unconstitutional. On February 23, Justice Grier wrote Buchanan a very long letter evidencing how thoroughly the president had won him over:

Your letter came to hand this morning. I have taken the liberty to shew it in confidence to our mutual friends Judge Wayne and the

Chief Justice. We fully appreciate and concur in your views as to the desirableness at this time of having an expression of the court on this troublesome question. With their concurrence, I will give you in confidence the history of the case before us, with the probable result.

At this point, Buchanan knew he had the ear of four Justices: Taney, Catron, Wayne, and Grier. Grier's letter continued on, spelled out the issues and the shifts in the Court's deliberations, beginning with the question of Scott's citizenship, and continuing:

After much discussion it was finally decided that the merits of the case might be satisfactorily decided without giving an opinion on the question of the Missouri Compromise; and the case was committed to Judge Nelson to write the opinion affirming the judgment of the court below but leaving both[105] those difficult questions untouched. But it appeared that our brothers who dissented from the majority, especially Justice McLean, were determined to come out with a long and labored dissent, including their opinions & arguments that on both the troublesome points, although not necessary to a decision of the case. In our opinion, both the points are in the case and may be legitimately considered.... A majority including all the judges south of Mason & Dixon's line agreeing in the result but not in their reasons – as the question will be thus forced upon us, I am anxious that it not appear that the line of latitude should mark the line of division in the court. I feel also that the opinion of the majority will fail of much of its effect if founded on clashing & inconsistent arguments. On conversation with the Chief Justice I have agreed to concur with him. Brother Wayne & myself will also use our endeavors to get brothers Daniels & Campbell & Catron to do the same.... There will be therefore six if not seven (perhaps Nelson will remain neutral) who will decide the compromise law of 1820 to be of noneffect.

Grier closed with an assurance that the opinion would not be delivered before Buchanan's inauguration and

We will not let any others of our brethren know anything about the

cause of our anxiety to produce this result, and although contrary to our usual practice, we have thought due to state to you in candor and confidence the real state of the matter.

Indeed, the president-elect had not needed Taney's whisper to tip him off about the result of the case. He knew the result, the vote count, and who would dissent, "in candor and confidence," two weeks before the ruling was announced.

It goes without saying that Justices giving a president inside information on their deliberations, and a president lobbying a Justice, at the request of another Justice, were extraordinary events. All the more so, since the president and the justices were secretly communicating on how to strike down Congressional power over the most critical issue of the day.

What would follow would be even more extraordinary.

VII

The Court Rules – and the Knives Come Out

The importance with which the Court regarded *Dred Scott v. Sandford* is reflected in the length of the ruling. By the standards of the day, it was a gargantuan ruling. The sixty other cases handed down that Term averaged just over six pages apiece. *Dred Scott*, with its concurrences and dissents, ran *241* pages!

Chief Justice Taney led off with his opinion, which he labelled the Opinion of the Court, and which he meant to bury the antislavery cause forever. We will focus on its key points, and then see how Justice Curtis answered them in his, the more important, dissent.

Taney: Free blacks as citizens

Taney first held that the trial court (and hence the Supreme Court) did not have jurisdiction, that is, the legal power to hear and decide the case.

Under the Constitution, federal diversity jurisdiction requires that the lawsuit be between "citizens" of different states. Taney argued that Dred Scott, and indeed all free blacks, were not citizens of states where they resided. They were not citizens nor aliens, just residents.

Even if the state in question regarded them as its citizens, Taney argued, federal courts could not recognize this in construing provisions of the U.S. Constitution, which had created a new "political family."

And why would free blacks be excluded from that "family?" Here, and elsewhere in the opinion, Taney lumped slaves in with free men, and used language designed to be provocative:

They had for more than a century before been regarded as beings of an inferior order, and altogether unfit to associate with the white race, either in social or political relations; and so far inferior, that they had no rights which the white man was bound to respect; and that the negro might justly and lawfully be reduced to slavery for his benefit. He was bought and sold, and treated as an ordinary article of merchandise and traffic, whenever a profit could be made by it. This opinion was at that time fixed and universal in the civilized portion of the white race. It was regarded as an axiom in morals as well as in politics….

Yes, Taney acknowledged, the Declaration of Independence had proclaimed that "all men are created equal," but when the Constitution was drafted this could not have been seen as referring to black Americans: "The general words above quoted would seem to embrace the whole human family, and if they were used in a similar instrument at this day would be so understood. But it is too clear for dispute, that the enslaved African race were not intended to be included, and formed no part of the people who framed and adopted this declaration…." As a young attorney, Taney had invoked the Declaration, asserting that in the day when slavery was ended "we can point without a blush to the language held in the Declaration of Independence."[106] That was then, this was now; he did not consider the possibility that the Framers' thinking might be closer to his youthful opinions than to his views in 1857.

Taney then invoked Article IV, section 2 of the Constitution, which states "the citizens of each state shall be entitled to all privileges and immunities of citizens in the several states," essentially forbidding any state to discriminate against citizens of other states. Given that command, Taney argued, the slaveowning states would never have agreed to free blacks being "citizens" for federal purposes:

For if they were so received, and entitled to the privileges and immunities of citizens, it would exempt them from the operation of the special laws and from the police regulations which they considered to be necessary for their own safety. It would give to persons of the negro race, who were recognized as citizens in any one State of the Union, the right to enter every other State whenever they pleased, singly or in companies, without pass or passport, and without obstruction, to sojourn there as long as they pleased, to go where they pleased at every hour of the day or night without molestation, unless they committed some violation of law for which a white man would be punished; and it would give them the full liberty of speech in public and in private upon all subjects upon which its own citizens might speak; to hold public meetings upon political affairs, and to keep and carry arms wherever they went. And all of this would be done in the face of the subject race of the same color, both free and slaves, and inevitably producing discontent and insubordination among them, and endangering the peace and safety of the State.

It is impossible, it would seem to believe that the great men of the slaveholding States, who took so large a share in framing the Constitution of the United States, and exercised so much influence in procuring its adoption, could have been so forgetful or regardless of their own safety and the safety of those who trusted and confided in them.

(Taney was again being anachronistic here: most of the regulations he cited were unknown in 1789, when the Constitution was ratified, and when slave codes commonly applied only to slaves. Louisiana Territory's first slave code, dating to 1806, had no restrictions on free blacks' movement, speech and meetings. The only restriction on their arms-bearing was a requirement that they carry proof of their freedom while carrying arms).[107]

Taney: Could Congress prohibit slavery in the territories?

Taney then proceeded to key issues, the first being whether Congress could prohibit slavery in the territories. Congress had done so for decades, and Article IV of the Constitution empowered Congress "to dispose of and make all needful rules and regulations respecting the territory or other property belonging to the United States." The power of Congress to make any rules it considered "needful" was the broadest grant of power to be found in the Constitution; after all, it deals with land that the government actually owns.

But Taney found a way around the wording. At the time the

Constitution was drafted, he pointed out, the United States possessed the Northwest Territories, western lands ceded to the Continental Congress by Virginia, Massachusetts, New York and Connecticut. Taney ruled that the Constitution's reference to "the territory" meant only *this* territory, not to all territories, and thus not territories later formed from the 1803 Louisiana Purchase.

> *The counsel for the plaintiff has laid much stress upon that article in the Constitution which confers on Congress the power "to dispose of and make all needful rules and regulations respecting the territory or other property belonging to the United States;" but, in the judgment of the court, that provision has no bearing on the present controversy, and the power there given ... was intended to be confined, to the territory which at that time belonged to, or was claimed by, the United States, and was within their boundaries as settled by the treaty with Great Britain, and can have no influence upon a territory afterwards acquired from a foreign Government. It was a special provision for a known and particular territory, and to meet a present emergency, and nothing more.*

The clause, he added, "does not speak of any territory, nor of Territories, but uses language which, according to its legitimate meaning, points to a particular thing," that is, the Northwest Territory. Only there did Congress have broad power to enact any "needful rules and regulations."

With those words, Taney had ended the possibility of Congressional compromise over the slavery issue. There could be no "we'll give you a slave territory, if you give us a free territory."

We do not know if Senator Stephen Douglas was in the courtroom as Taney spoke, but certainly many of Douglas' most powerful supporters were. So far, they had good reason to be delighted with Taney's work. Douglas – who would in a few years face Lincoln as a presidential contender – was the foremost advocate of "popular sovereignty" – don't have Congress decide whether a territory is free or slave, let the people of a territory decide that question for themselves. All that Taney had said to this point was consistent with that: he had written Douglas' political platform into the Constitution.

They rejoiced too early. Taney was just hitting his stride.

Taney: Could a territorial legislature prohibit slavery?

Congress could not, Taney observed, violate the Bill of Rights in the course of governing a territory.

For example, no one, we presume, will contend that Congress can make any law in a Territory respecting the establishment of religion, or the free exercise thereof, or abridging the freedom of speech or of the press, or the right of the people of the Territory peaceably to assemble, and to petition the Government for the redress of grievances.

Taney pointed out that Bill of Rights also guaranteed a citizen in his property; the Fifth Amendment commanded that no person "be deprived of his life, liberty, or property, without due process of law." Taney continued:

And an act of Congress which deprives a citizen of the United States of his liberty or property, merely because he came himself or brought his property into a particular Territory of the United States, and who had committed no offence against the laws, could hardly be dignified with the name of due process of law.

By "property," Taney of course meant slaves. So far so good, the Douglas men might have reflected. Slaves are property, and Congress cannot take property away without due process of law. A second reason why Congress cannot restrict slavery in the territories. Very nice for Douglas' platform!

Then Taney dropped his bombshell:

And if Congress itself cannot do this — if it is beyond the powers conferred on the Federal Government — it will be admitted, we presume, that it could not authorize a Territorial Government to exercise them. It could confer no power on any local Government, established by its authority, to violate the provisions of the Constitution.

Having killed Congressional power over slavery, Taney had just killed popular sovereignty as well! *Neither* Congress *nor* territorial legislatures could restrict slavery. *There was no longer such a thing as a free territory, and there was nothing anybody could do to prevent this.* The Douglas men in the courtroom must have been aghast at Taney's words.

The remainder of the day was consumed by reading of opinions by Justices who joined with all or most of Taney's opinion. The two dissenters, McLean and Curtis, read their opinions on the next day. Of the two, Curtis was by far the more effective.

Curtis: Free blacks as citizens

Was Dred Scott a citizen, within the meaning of the Constitution? Yes, Curtis argued. The Articles of Confederation, which preceded the Constitution, had treated any citizen of a confederated state as a citizen of the United States. A citizen of a state had united was a citizen of the United States. Indeed, he pointed out, Article II, section four, of the Constitution proved that the Framers saw citizenship under the Constitution as a continuation of citizenship under the Articles. That section required that the president be a natural-born citizen or a "citizen of the United States, at the time of the adoption of this Constitution."

Were free blacks citizens of the United States under the Articles of Confederation? Curtis had the answer:

> *At the time of the ratification of the Articles of Confederation, all free native-born inhabitants of the States of New Hampshire, Massachusetts, New York, New Jersey, and North Carolina, though descended from African slaves, were not only citizens of those States, but such of them as had the other necessary qualifications possessed the franchise of electors, on equal terms with other citizens.*

Moreover, the Articles of Confederation had a "privileges and immunities" clause, similar to the one placed in the Constitution, forbidding states to discriminate against free inhabitants of other states. Curtis pointed out that the Continental Congress had voted down, 8-2, a proposal to limit this to free white inhabitants.

Free blacks were thus clearly citizens of the United States under the Articles of Confederation. Can we believe, Curtis asked, that the Constitution had been meant, by silence, to strip these people of their citizenship?

Curtis: Could Congress prohibit slavery in the territories?

Did the Constitution give Congress power over the territories other than the Northwest Territory? Curtis' answer was, yes. When the Constitution was framed, it was expected that Congress would acquire other territory. "But this North-western Territory was not the only territory, the soil and jurisdiction whereof were then understood to have been ceded to the United States." South Carolina had ceded territory to Congress and it was expected that North Carolina and Georgia would do so as well. The Framers had meant Congress to have broad power over all territories, not just the pre-existing Northwest Territory.

Any other conclusion would involve the assumption that a subject of the gravest national concern, respecting which the small States felt so much jealousy that it had been almost an insurmountable obstacle to the formation of the Confederation, and as to which all the States had deep pecuniary and political interests, and which had been so recently and constantly agitated, was nevertheless overlooked; or that such a subject was not overlooked, but designedly left unprovided for, though it was manifestly a subject of common concern, which belonged to the care of the General Government, and adequate provision for which could not fail to be deemed necessary and proper.

Was there any reason, Curtis asked, to believe that the Framers wanted to restrict Congressional power over territories to the

Northwest Territory? Was there any indication in the historical record that they meant to so limit it? He could find none.

Did the Fifth Amendment's restriction on deprivation of property without due process of law prevent Congress, or a territory, from restricting entry of slaves? No, Curtis reasoned. Slavery was a special case. "Slavery, being contrary to natural right, is created only by municipal [*i.e.*, local, statutory] law. This is not only plain in itself, and agreed by all writers on the subject, but is inferable from the Constitution, and has been explicitly declared by this court." One state or territory might recognize slavery, and another forbid it. If a slaveholder moved into the latter, he had to accept the legal consequence that his slaves became free.

For these reasons, I am of opinion that so much of the several acts of Congress as prohibited slavery and involuntary servitude within that part of the Territory of Wisconsin lying north of thirty-six degree thirty minutes north latitude, and west of the river Mississippi, were constitutional and valid laws.

Curtis' dissent was powerful; Taney concluded that he must counter it, even if that required him to violate his own Court's rules.

Taney strikes back – and his effort backfires

The normally-scrupulous Chief Justice now took some actions that were clearly improper. The culture of the Court was then more verbal than written. Briefs were rare, days of oral argument were the norm, opinions were read in full from the bench. The reading of the opinion was key, and Rule 42 of the Rules of the Supreme Court required that a Justice must "immediately upon the delivery thereof" turn his opinion over to the clerk for printing.[108]

Taney didn't hand his over. Instead, he began adding sections to it meant to counter the dissents. Justice Curtis later estimated that eighteen pages, or *nearly one-third* of what became Taney's printed opinion reflected additions that he made after-the-fact. "No one can read them," he noted, "without perceiving that they are in reply to my opinion."[109] So extensive were the revisions that Taney labored over them for two months.

This, of course, gave Taney an unfair advantage over the dissenters, who followed the rules and promptly gave their opinions to the clerk. He could try to produce an opinion that met their objections, while they would have no chance to answer his additions.

But Taney's delay had an unintended consequence. The dissenters filed their opinions, and, thinking the case was over, released copies of their dissents to the press, which lost no time in reprinting them. Taney's "new and revised" opinion stayed a secret for two months. For those two months, the dissents were the documents that dominated the news, while Taney labored in secret to rewrite the majority opinion. *Dred Scott* would have been highly controversial in any event. But the fact that from March until May, 1857, the dissents were public knowledge while the majority opinion was not, contributed fuel to the developing firestorm. As the *Macon Observer* wrote in early April:

> *The opinion of the Court, as read on the 5th inst., by Chief Justice Taney, has not yet been filed; but, I learn, the venerable Judge will be ready to file it this day.... The dissenting opinions of Justices McLean and Curtis were filed on the 9th, but copies of the same had been previously furnished for the press, and they were both printed and published in Boston, New York, &c.... Justices Curtis and McLean stole a march upon their brethren of the court, by a prompt promulgation of their dissenting opinions, which have reached thousands of readers in the northern states, who will never see Howard's Reports* [the Court's official publication].[110]

Taney's tactic had another consequence. *Dred Scott* had been the last case of the Term, and Justice Curtis had gone home to Massachusetts for the summer. As the weeks passed with no word of the printed decision being released, he started to become suspicious. In early April, a month after the opinions had been read, he wrote the clerk of the court to ask for a copy of Taney's opinion as soon it had been typeset. The clerk replied that Taney had forbade him to release copies to anyone before the volume in which it was contained was printed, bound, and released. Curtis wrote again, saying that surely such an order does not extend to members of the Court, and the clerk replied he had checked with Taney, and yes, it did.

Curtis wrote to Taney for clarification, and the normally-polite Taney responded coldly that Curtis would be entitled to it if he wanted it to carry out his duties, but that was not Curtis' purpose. "I understand you as not desiring or intending to use it for that purpose. On the contrary, you announced from the bench that you regarded the opinion as extra-judicial, and not binding upon you or any one else. And if the opinion of the Court is desired by the judge, not to aid him in the discharge of his public duties, but for some other unexplained purpose, I do not see that his position in relation to a copy of the opinion differs in any respect from that of any other person."[111]

The postal fight between the two went on for two months, with Taney complaining that Curtis had released his dissent to the press, and while the Court had been attacked by newspapers in the past, "this is the first instance in the history of the Supreme Court in which the assault was commenced by the publication of the opinion of a dissenting judge." The "avowed purpose" of Curtis' dissent, Taney alleged, "was to impair its [Taney's opinion's] authority and discredit it as a judicial decision," and its release to the press had encouraged attacks "by political partisans whose prejudices and passions were already enlisted against the constitutional principles affirmed by the court."[112] (Taney's anger may have been fueled by rumors circulating in the press that the dissenters had given copies of their opinions to newspapers before, instead of after, the dissents were read).[113]

The nastiness of Taney's reaction was likely driven by his view of his *Dred Scott* ruling. Taney, like his mentor Andrew Jackson, saw sectionalism, North vs. South, as the principal threat to the Union.[114] By 1857, sectionalism was all about slavery. Taney undoubtedly saw his *Dred Scott* opinion as rescuing the Union from a deadly threat, by taking slavery in the territories outside the domain of politics, and Justice Curtis as seeking to thwart this rescue by any means, fair or foul. In Taney's mind, he himself was a patriot, a Unionist, which made Curtis something of a traitor.

Ironically, Taney's efforts improperly to perfect his opinion, and the consequent delay in its release, ensured that *Dred Scott* would heighten rather than reduce sectional divisions in the country, and contribute to the breakdown of the Union.

Speaking of unintended consequences….

VIII

The Chaffees' Role Becomes National News

Rep. Chaffee was certainly appalled at the Supreme Court decision, but he and his wife Irene must have been relieved that their role, as the Scott family's real owners, had not been revealed.[115]

That happy state of affairs lasted about a week.

The pro-slavery press "outs" the Chaffees

Congress was then out of session, and Dr. Chaffee was back in Springfield, Massachusetts, where the local press consisted of the pro-slavery *Springfield Argus* and the anti-slavery *Springfield Republican*. To Chaffee's shock, only a few days after the Court ruled, the *Argus* proclaimed that he and Irene were Dred Scott's real owners. The *Argus* went out of business a few months later, and no copy of its article survives. [116] We can, however, reconstruct its coverage from other newspapers that reprinted its articles verbatim, a common practice of the time. The longest such article appeared in the March 17, 1857 edition of the Syracuse, N.Y. *Daily Courier*:

From the following article, which we copy from the Springfield Argus, it appears that Dred Scott and his family became, by the recent decision of the Supreme Court, the property of the wife of Dr. Chaffee, the Republican Member of Congress from the Springfield (Mass.) district:

It may perhaps astonish some of our rabid Fremonters [Republicans], to know that the late decision in the Supreme Court remanding to slavery Dred Scott and his family, declaring the unconstitutionality of the Missouri Compromise, and establishing the right to slave-holders to carry their chattels [personal property] into Northern States without affecting their security in them – was obtained on behalf of our present honorable member of Congress.

The facts are simply these: Some years ago, Dr. Chaffee, then a widower, married the widow of Dr. Emerson, of Missouri, who had died, leaving to his wife and only daughter a considerable slave property. Among those slaves was Dred Scott and his family. ... The suit, thus brought, was defended by the administrator of the estate on behalf, and with the consent of the wife of Dr. Chaffee and her daughter, who were the heirs at law. The decision of the bench that Dred Scott was not a citizen of the U.S. and could not sue in the U.S. Court, has remanded him and his family to the chattlehood [status of property] *of Mrs. Chaffee. What does the Doctor propose to do with this [illegible] property? Does he consent to the prosecution, and under cover of his wife's crinoline, propose to keep good friends with the Black Republicans, by saying that he has nothing to do with her estate, and at the same times enjoy with her the benefit of the estate, which does not stop with the unfortunate Dred and his family?*[117]

The *Argus* ran follow-up stories, although again none of these survive. From other newspapers' descriptions of the *Argus* series, it seems Dr. Chaffee originally denied everything. When, a few months later, the *Syracuse Daily Courier* praised the *Argus*'s coverage, it referred to "Dr. Chaffee, writhing under the scathing exposures of the *Argus*" and noted that when Chaffee protested his innocence, "[t]he *Argus* followed this up with facts and statements fully authenticated, proving the falseness of this excuse, and finally copied from a St. Louis paper a history of the case [*i.e.*, the state freedom suit], more than proving all that had previously been charged upon Dr. Chaffee."[118]

It did not remain a local story. The *Syracuse Daily Courier* later claimed that "The telegraph has carried the faithful message to every part of the country, and the black Republican trader in the flesh and blood of the illustrious Dred Scott, is known by this time to every gentleman who will be honored by a seat with him in the next Congress."[119] In Massachusetts, the *Pittsfield Sun* jabbed, "It seems that while Dr. Chaffee was "shrieking for freedom," and receiving the support of his Black Republican friends for Congress, he was at the same time prosecuting a suit for the recovery of a runaway negro! Admirable consistency!!"[120]

The story received such widespread publicity that Stephen Douglas could invoke it during his Senate campaign against Lincoln, with the audience knowing enough to be amused by the jab. To Lincoln's claim that the *Dred Scott* case was, together with the Kansas-Nebraska Act, a pro-slavery conspiracy, Douglas replied:

> *He ought to have known that the at time of the passage of the Nebraska bill the Dred Scott case had not yet been taken up to the Supreme Court; it was still pending in the district courts of Missouri. It had been begun by Dred Scott, and we had not possession of him because he was in the hands of abolitionist friends. (Laughter.) Mr. Lincoln, as an abolitionist, might have known that if Dred Scott lost his case in the district courts of Missouri that he intended to appeal to the Supreme Court of the United States; but I never did, and had no means of learning the fact.* [121]

(In the Lincoln-Douglas debates that followed, Douglas became more explicit, twice explicitly naming the Chaffees, sarcastically termed "Lincoln's friends," as Dred Scott's owners).[122]

Chaffee's supporters rally in his defence

Dr. Chaffee's supporters quickly entered the fray. The first defense came in the *Springfield Republican*, which on March 14, 1857, ran two articles on the subject. The first took the form of a letter to the editor:

To the Editor of the Republican:

The opposition press and common street rumor bring me strange reports, affecting the position of Dr. Chaffee in the Dred Scott decision ... I, as one of his friends and supporters, have presumed to ask for more light on this subject.

Does Mrs. Chaffee, as the widow of the late Dr. Emerson of Missouri, have any interest in the ownership of Dred Scott and his family, whose suit for freedom was defended by the administrator of the estate? and has she any power now, or will she have any at some future time, over the said Scott and his family? Is the administrator who defended the suit a brother of Mrs. Chaffee? and did he act with her knowledge and consent, or on her behalf? Does the estate of Dr. Emerson cover other slave property that will hereafter accrue to Mrs. Chaffee, or her daughter? and does either of them own other slaves? Also, are there any facts to show that the system of slavery is repugnant to the feelings of Dr. Chaffee, and his family, and that they are unwilling to own slaves should any hereafter be divided to them?

The second article carried the newspaper's defense of Dr. Chaffee. It began by agreeing that defendant John F. A. Sanford was indeed Mrs. Chaffee's brother, then quoted from the agreed statement of facts to the effect that the Scotts had been sold to Sanford prior to suit, calling these "common and well known public facts." It continued: "Our own opinion is that the case was made up at St. Louis, for the purpose of testing this question, and getting just the opinions that the majority of the court has given, and that Mr. Sanford, who has acted as the defendant, has no active interest or personal motive in the case."[123]

Massachusetts newspapers like the *Lowell Daily Citizen and News* took their cue from the *Republican*, running the agreed statement of facts and arguing that Sanford bought the Scott family from Dr. Emerson before Emerson's death, so that "Dr. Chaffee and his wife have no more to do with them than the 'man (and woman) in the moon.'"[124]

Dr. Chaffee defends himself

Dr. Chaffee was eventually forced to explain himself. What seems unusual is that in these defenses, Chaffee did not claim what the stipulated facts had claimed – that Sanford was the owner of the Scott family, and had purchased them from Dr. Emerson. That position would have left Dr. Chaffee's and Irene's hands perfectly clean but it was simply indefensible.

His first statement was given to the *Springfield Republican* and reprinted in the *New York Daily Tribune*. Chaffee began with a note he had only recently seen the *Republican*'s previous article, adding:

I have lived to little purpose if, after more than twenty years' service in the Anti-Slavery cause, it not necessary that I should put in a formal disclaimer of my own participation in the sin and crime of slave-holding.... [T]here is no earthly consideration that could induce me to exercise proprietorship in any human being; for I regard Slavery as a sin against God and a crime against man.

In the case of Dred Scott, the defendant [John F. A. Sanford] *was and is the only person who had or has any power in the matter, and neither myself nor any member of my family were consulted in relation to or even knew of the existence until after it was noticed for trial, when we learned of it in an accidental way – and I agree with you that if I had possessed of any power or influence in the case, and failed to use it then I should have been "guilty of treason to my professions and betrayal of the confidence of my constituents."*

But possessed of no power to control – refused all right to influence the course of the defendant in the cause – and all the while feeling and openly expressing the fullest sympathy with Dred Scott and his family, in their efforts to secure their just rights to freedom – no man in this land feels more deeply the intense wrong done, not only to them but to the whole people, by the monstrous decisions of the majority of the United States Supreme Court. And if in the distribution of the estate, of which this decision affirms these human beings to be part, I or mine consent to receive any part of the thirty pieces of silver, then, and not till then, let the popular judgment, as well as the public press, fix on me the mark of a traitor to my conscience, as well at the true rights of our common humanity.[125]

The *New York Daily Tribune*, the most widely-circulated daily newspaper in the country, went further, telling its readers that Dr. Chaffee *was utterly ignorant that Dred Scott existed, down to the present year; and even Mrs. Chaffee, to whom he had been a servant, supposed him dead throughout last year, and was only apprised in February, 1857, that the Dred Scott about whom the great law suit was going on in the Supreme Court, was the slave of her deceased husband. (He has been left to himself since Dr. Emerson's death).*[126]

The date of Chaffee's alleged discovery is quite unclear. "Noticed for trial" presumably meant set for argument or re-argument in the Supreme Court. The Court granted re-argument on May 12, 1856, with the argument beginning on December 15, 1856. But the *Herald Tribune* article places his (or to be exact, Mrs. Chaffee's) discovery in February of the next year, 1857. Depending upon which date is correct, then, Dr. Chaffee would have had anywhere from a few weeks to ten months' warning before the Supreme Court actually ruled. That Chaffee stated he was refused all right to control the case suggests that he made such an effort; unfortunately, he never gave any further details.

Chaffee did not have the last word. The *Argus* returned to the attack, again in articles we know only from other newspapers:

The questions which now arise are: has not Dr. C. received the benefits arising from the sale of those negroes? Would he not have suffered pecuniary loss had the suit been decided for the plaintiff? Was not the Dr.'s influence with his wife and brother-in-law sufficiently powerful to have stopped this suit by refunding the monies arising from their sale, and giving them their freedom without a trial? and is not the Dr. receiving benefit either from slave labor or from monies accruing from the sale of slaves. We say nothing as to the morality of thus holding slaves, or of using monies acquired, but if such really is the case, is not a little inconsistent to be shrieking for freedom and harping on the wrongs of the slave? Will the Doctor explain? Springfield Argus.[127]

Newspapers soon uncovered records of the Scott's state freedom suits, and the *Milwaukee Daily News* demanded additional explanation:

Mrs. Emerson (now Mrs. Chaffee) leased these slaves out for hire during the first year after her husband's death. She has never manumitted them nor has she ever sold them. She did, however, propose to sell them in 1846, and this occasioned the instigation of the suit for freedom.

Mr. Chaffee says that neither himself nor any member of his family knew of the suit until the case was noticed for trial, when it came to his knowledge accidentally. Now, the record of this case shows that suit was [illegible – filed?] in the St. Louis Circuit Court against Mrs. Chaffee herself, who had personal service of the writ on the 7th day of April, 1846. Moreover, the same record shows that she has defended that case in the courts of Missouri for more than ten years, where the case of Dred Scott v. Irene Emerson (Mrs. Chaffee) is still pending.... The truth is, Mr. Sanford never had anything to do with these slaves, except as the executor of Dr. Emerson, or agent of Mrs. Chaffee.

. . . . . .

Had Mrs. Chaffee surrendered her claim to Dred Scott [illegible] the first suit was brought, it would have effectually liberated that slave. Nay, had she been satisfied with the verdict of the Missouri jury, that declared Dred Scott a free man, instead of appealing to the Supreme Court of the State, the slave would now have enjoyed the inestimable privilege which Mr. Chaffee admits he deserves.[128]

The *Pittsfield Sun* was more blunt:

Dred brought his suit for freedom ten years ago, and has spent $500 in prosecuting it—This money he has been obliged to raise by overwork, and now at an advanced age finds himself minus his cash and his liberty too. – Poor old African! in falling into the hands of a Massachusetts freedom-shrieker his chains were not loosened, but his old body and soul are clutched with the same tenacity as though he were the property of some border ruffian. Why don't the Hon. Dr. Chaffee free his slave? Perhaps the Sentinel can inform the public on this point.[129]

The Scott family finally gains its freedom

The *Sun* didn't know it, but that thought had already occurred to Dr. Chaffee. On April 1, 1857, Chaffee had written Montgomery Blair, who had argued Dred Scott's case before the Supreme Court:

CONFIDENTIAL

Since the decision of the case Dred Scott vs. J.F.A. Sanford has so profoundly stirred the public mind and some of the pro slavery newspapers have attributed to me an interest in the persons claimed as slaves, my wife, as the widow of the late doct. Emerson, and the sole legatee of the will, desires to know whether she has the legal power and right to emancipate the Dred Scott family . . . If she has this right [illegible] if you [illegible: would forward?] the necessary papers, she will cheerfully execute them.

May I not hope to hear from you at an early day.[130]

The response cannot be located, but ten days later Chaffee again wrote Blair, thanking him for his response and adding:

I perceive by a communication in the Mis. Republican of the 5th or 6th inst., that Mrs. C. is the overseer of the "Scott" family – that may be true or not – if so I am as you may well imagine, anxious to free myself and family from the odious relationship. If not too much trouble, my dear sir, I beg of you to forward to me the [illegible] of my wife's ownership & the necessary papers for the [illegible] of the freedom of the Dred Scott family – my whole soul utterly loathes and abhors the whole system of slavery & not only myself but my family must be cleared from it.[131]

Blair forwarded the Doctor's correspondence to Roswell Field, Scott's St. Louis attorney, who replied that Mrs. Chaffee and her daughter had full power over the Scotts, enclosing a draft deed transferring the Scotts to their friend Taylor Blow, and explaining that "Our law requires that all deeds of emancipation be acknowledged or proved before the circuit court; and it has been thought advisable to effect the object by transfer to a citizen here who is ready to go into circuit court to make the necessary acknowledgement."[132] The letter adds an interesting human element to the tale:

Dred desires that the copy of the will of Dr. Emerson may be returned to him. He was enabled to procure it with a dollar presented to him by Judge Catron of the United States Supreme Court, who, in his recent visit here to hold the Circuit Court, sent for Dred and treated him with much friendly conversation and Christian sympathy, showing that in the opinion of the judge if they were not fellow citizens, they were at least fellow men. Dred wishes that the copy of the will may be returned so that he may keep it as a memorial of Judge Catron's kindness.[133]

The deed was executed – an event delayed by Mrs. Chaffee's attendance at John Sanford's death[134] -- and Chaffee transmitted it with a request: "I desire now, in conclusion of the case, to be privately informed of the act of emancipation, but that there should be no publicity given the subject beyond strict legal necessity."[135]

On May 26, 1857, Taylor Blow appeared in the St. Louis Circuit Court and formally manumitted the Scott family. After 15 years, their quest for freedom was at an end.

Their role in history was only beginning.

Dr. Chaffee's letter to Montgomery Blair, the Scotts' Supreme attorney, seeking advice on how to free the family. (Library of Congress, Manuscript Division, Blair Family Papers)

Mr Sanford's Mental condition
is such that he can give no infor
-mation on the subject and she
is desirous, if within her power
of washing her hands of all partici
-pancy in the matter –

If she has this right and
power, if you would forward
the necessary papers, she will
cheerfully execute them –

May I not hope to hear from
you at an early day.
Very respectfully
Your Obt Servt
C. C. Chaffee

IX

Dred Scott's Enduring Legacy

The Court's ruling aggravated rather than neutralized the sectional conflict. It aroused a "storm of anger" in the North;[136] Lincoln's secretaries later wrote that, while the conflict in Kansas had agitated the public temper, *Dred Scott* "suddenly doubled its intensity."[137] Fifty years after the decision, D. W. Grissom, a St. Louis newspaper editor, described the ruling as "arousing an anti-slavery feeling in the North beyond that produced by any other case except 'Uncle Tom's Cabin.'"[138]

The *New York Times* wrote that "the country was convulsed" by the ruling, [139] while the *New York Daily Tribune* referred to the "outrageous opinion delivered by Chief Justice Taney in the name of the slaveholding Judges of the Supreme Court."[140] Smaller newspapers joined in. The *Madison Daily State Journal* described the ruling as one "in which the octogenarian judge falsified history and subverts the fundamental principles of law in his zeal to serve the slavery propagandists."[141] In Iowa, the *Fairfield Ledger* denounced the "contemptible decision" that "endeavors to turn this country into a mere machine for the protection and perpetuation of human slavery."[142]

In the West, where the territorial question was more immediate, the ruling had even more powerful effects. A Wisconsin newspaper informed readers that two of Michigan's four Democratic newspapers had abandoned that party and that one "pitches into the decision with even greater fury than many of its Republican contemporaries."[143]

Dred Scott had a direct and powerful impact on the affairs of two rising political figures.

Dred Scott and the rise of Abraham Lincoln

Abraham Lincoln, then "virtually unknown,"[144] seized upon the decision, arguing that *Dred Scott* and the Kansas-Nebraska Act were the work of a pro-slavery conspiracy embracing all three branches of government. In his "House Divided" speech, accepting his nomination as a Senate candidate, he charged:

> *Let anyone who doubts carefully contemplate that now almost complete legal combination -- piece of machinery, so to speak – compounded of the Nebraska doctrine and the Dred Scott decision.... We cannot know that all these exact adaptations are the result of preconcert. But when we see a lot of framed timbers, different portions of which we know have been gotten out at different times and by different workmen ... and we see these timbers joined together, and see that they exactly make the frame of a house or mill... in such a case we find it impossible not to believe that Stephen and Franklin and Roger and James all understood one another from the beginning, and all worked from a common plan or draft drawn up before the first blow was struck.*[145]

The first names given were those of Stephen Douglas, former president Franklin Pierce, Chief Justice Roger Taney, and president James Buchanan; Lincoln was charging that all had conspired to impose universal legalized slavery on the country. He warned that *Dred Scott* might not only make slavery legal in free territories, but also in free states, a cry already being voiced by others. In Illinois, Senator Lyman Trumbull argued that "Next, they will deny the power of the people when they form a State constitution to exclude it; and that such is the next step to be taken is manifest from the Dred Scott decision."[146] A Massachusetts newspaper editorialized that "the Dred Scott decision makes slavery as legal in Massachusetts as in any other state or territory."[147]

(This was not quite legally correct: *Dred Scott* had focused upon *Congressional* power over *territories*, not the power of a state over its own residents. On the other hand, given how the Court had stretched the law to reach its desired result, it was possible to fear that it might manage to apply a comparable limitation to states).

Dred Scott of course struck at Lincoln's position on slavery, but he easily sidestepped the blow by suggesting that the Supreme Court had been wrong before, and had reversed itself; it was no disloyalty to the Constitution to hope that the Court might do so in this case.[148]

The election of 1858 saw Senate rivals Abraham Lincoln and Stephen Douglas pitted against each other; the actual race was for control of the Illinois legislature, which at that time chose its U.S. senators. At first, they travelled Illinois separately presenting their cases; at length they agreed to seven joint appearances. These Lincoln-Douglas Debates focused almost entirely upon slavery and related issues, and *Dred Scott* predictably played a major role in them. In fact, toward the end of the first debate, at Ottawa, Illinois, one Douglas supporter cried out to Lincoln, "Give us something besides Dred Scott!" Lincoln shot back, "Now, no doubt, you would rather hear something that don't hurt you." His riposte met with cheers and applause.[149] By the end of the debates, either Lincoln or Douglas had explicitly discussed *Dred Scott* nineteen times, atop frequent references to its principles.[150]

After losing that election, Lincoln set his eye on the presidency. To achieve that goal, he must become more than an Illinois candidate; he must prove he had a place on the national stage, and become competitive against established national anti-slavery leaders such as William Seward – U.S. Senator, and former governor of New York, and Salmon Chase – former Senator, now governor of Ohio. It was a tall order for an uneducated western politician, whose most recent experiences as a candidate involved losing a Senate race and losing a bid at becoming the Republicans' vice-presidential candidate.

Lincoln got his opportunity when he was invited to address a New York City gathering in February, 1860, a speech that became known from its location as his Cooper Union address. Lincoln chose as his target the major theme of *Dred Scott*, Congressional power over the territories, and he focused upon a statement made by Senator Douglas, that "Our fathers, when they framed the government under which we live, understood this question [slavery] just as well, and even better, than we do now."

Lincoln began his address by asking, who might those fathers be? The logical choice was the 39 framers who signed the Constitution. Then he traced the actions of those 39 in early Congresses which voted to forbid or at least to restrict slavery in the territories. The prohibition of slavery in the Northwest Territory was a prime example, but there had also been votes to limit slavery in Mississippi and Louisiana Territories, and the Missouri Compromise, which outlawed slavery in most of the Louisiana Purchase territories.

Lincoln's count: of the 39 framers, 23 had as legislators voted on whether to control slavery in territories, and had voted 21-2 in favor of the proposed restrictions. The remaining 16 Framers had not voted on the issue, but since they contained several persons known to be anti-slavery, and only one person possibly favorable to it, likely they, too, assumed that Congress could control territorial slavery.

The sum of the whole is, that of our thirty-nine fathers who framed the original Constitution, twenty-one – a clear majority of the whole – certainly understood that no proper division of local from federal authority, nor any part of the Constitution, forbade the federal government to control slavery in the federal territories; while all the rest probably had the same understanding. Such, unquestionably, was the understanding of our fathers who framed the original Constitution; and the text affirms that they understood the question "better than we." [Laughter and cheers].[151]

The Cooper Union address showed a new Lincoln, an advocate who could speak calmly and dispassionately, proving a conclusion by research and cold reason; there were no homespun analogies here. The newspapers loved the presentation; the *New York Times* praised it, and announced that it had ended with three rousing cheers from the audience; the *New York Daily Tribune* termed it "one of the happiest and most convincing political arguments ever made in this city."[152] Newspaper coverage was so extensive that within days 170,000 copies of the speech were in circulation.[153] A modern historian concludes, "Lincoln remade himself in New York on February 27, 1860. It is fair to say that never before or since in American history has a single speech so dramatically catapulted a candidate toward the White House."[154]

For Lincoln, then, *Dred Scott* was the gift that kept on giving. His future presidential opponent Stephen Douglas was not so fortunate.

Dred Scott and the destruction of Stephen Douglas

Dred Scott had ruled that Douglas' position on slavery (the people of a territory could outlaw it) was as unconstitutional as that of Lincoln (Congress could outlaw it). This necessarily limited Douglas in any attempts to criticize Lincoln for repudiating the ruling; Douglas himself was forced to find a way around the ruling.

Strategically, the case fatally undercut Douglas' candidacy. His support of popular sovereignty was a compromise position, one acceptable to pro-slavery forces only because it seemed the best they were likely to achieve in the real world. If Congress controlled the slavery issue, they could expect little now, with the House solidly anti-slavery and the Senate roughly tied, a situation that would only worsen with the passage of time. At least with popular sovereignty they could hope to move in sufficient slave-owning settlers to control a territorial legislature, an approach they were taking in Kansas. There was, in short, no better deal than popular sovereignty on the horizon and thus no better pro-slavery candidate than Douglas.

Then came *Dred Scott*. The Supreme Court did what Congress would never have done, it had opened *all* the territories to slavery.

Now, why should pro-slavery forces accept popular sovereignty, or Stephen Douglas? Why accept compromise, when you've already won?

Douglas was caught in a strategic dilemma. He could become acceptable to the slave states only by foreswearing popular sovereignty and endorsing universal territorial slavery, slavery even where the people of a territory didn't want it – but that position would demolish his candidacy in the free states.

Douglas tried to retain his compromise position with what became known as his "Freeport Doctrine" – slavery could only exist where legislation supported it, so the people of a territory could exclude slavery simply by refusing to enact a slave code.[155] In the second debate, at Freeport, Illinois, Lincoln asked Douglas:

Can the people of a United States territory, in any lawful way, against the wishes of any citizen of the United States, exclude slavery from their limits prior to the formation of a state constitution?[156]

Douglas answered:

Whatever the Supreme Court may thereafter decide as to the abstract question of whether slavery may go in under the Constitution or not, the people of a territory have a lawful means to admit it or exclude it as they please, for the reason that slavery cannot exist a day or an hour unless supported by local police regulations, furnishing remedies and a means of enforcing the right to hold slaves. Those local and police regulations can only be furnished by the local legislature. If the people of the territory are opposed to slavery, they will elect members to the legislature who will adopt unfriendly legislation to it.[157]

No slave code, no slavery. It was a facile answer, one that enabled Douglas to reconcile his popular sovereignty position with his call for acceptance of *Dred Scott*. It was a popular position in Illinois, and it is no wonder that Douglas kept his Senate seat.[158]

But it had a profound impact on the Presidential election two years later. Douglas had already alienated pro-slavery forces (and the Buchanan administration) by opposing a slavery-favorable constitution for Kansas, a constitution he felt went contrary to the Kansans' desires. Douglas' answer to *Dred Scott* took him beyond the pale. Fresh from their Supreme Court win, pro-slavery forces saw Douglas as having invented and popularized a way to cheat them of their triumph; in their eyes he went from champion to traitor. As Lincoln's secretaries later wrote, Douglas's Freeport Doctrine "became in the eyes of the South the unpardonable political heresy."[159]

The result was that in the election of 1860 the anti-Lincoln side hopelessly divided. The Democratic Party had to hold a second convention after the first deadlocked. The second convention nominated Douglas, whereupon southern Democratic leaders held their own convention, and nominated John C. Breckinridge. Breckinridge ran on a platform that began:

1. That the Government of a Territory organized by an act of Congress, is provisional and temporary; and during its existence, all citizens of the United States have an equal right to settle with their property in the Territory, without their rights, either of person or property, being destroyed or impaired by Congressional or Territorial legislation.

2. That it is the duty of the Federal Government, in all its departments, to protect, when necessary, the rights of persons and property in the Territories, and wherever else its Constitutional authority extends.[160]

The first was a complete endorsement of *Dred Scott*; the second a rejection of popular sovereignty, and a call for Congress to enact a territorial slave code, *i.e*, to force slavery upon unwilling territories.

(To further confuse things, John Bell was nominated by a new Constitutional Union party, whose platform largely ignored slavery).

When election day came, the anti-Lincoln votes numbered 60%, yet, because they were divided three ways, Lincoln won the presidency. Douglas, hitherto the viable candidate of the largest American political party, and whom Lincoln feared would even strip away Republican support,[161] was crushed in the Electoral College 180-12. A historian writes:

It is impossible to exaggerate the effect of the Dred Scott decision. It destroyed Douglas. ... Douglas was forced to fall back upon the doctrine of unfriendly legislation which he had original promulgated in 1850. This enabled Lincoln to reply: "Judge Douglas says that a thing may be lawfully driven from a place where it has a lawful right to be." Upon this issue, the South deserted Douglas and the Democratic party divided.[162]

On March 4, 1861, four years almost to the day after he handed down *Dred Scott*, Chief Justice Roger Taney administered the oath of office to Abraham Lincoln.

Lincoln's election is, however, only part of the legacy of *Dred Scott*.

The Civil War amendments to the Constitution

The 13th, 14th, and 15th amendments to the Constitution are attributable in large part to *Dred Scott*. The 13th Amendment, proposed by Congress and ratified by the states in 1866, outlawed slavery: "Neither slavery nor involuntary servitude, except as a punishment for crime whereof the party shall have been duly convicted, shall exist within the United States, or any place subject to their jurisdiction." In nine years, slavery had gone from being constitutionally protected to being constitutionally prohibited.

The 15th Amendment guaranteed the voting rights of black Americans: "The right of citizens of the United States to vote shall not be denied or abridged by the United States or by any state on account of race, color, or previous condition of servitude."

But the most direct assault on Taney's ruling came in section one of the 14th Amendment, proposed by Congress in 1866 and ratified in 1868. That section was directly aimed at obliterating what remained of *Dred Scott*:

All persons born or naturalized in the United States, and subject to the jurisdiction thereof, are citizens of the United States and of the state wherein they reside. No state shall make or enforce any law which shall abridge the privileges or immunities of citizens of the United States; nor shall any state deprive any person of life, liberty, or property, without due process of law; nor deny to any person within its jurisdiction the equal protection of the laws.

The first sentence wiped out *Dred Scott*'s holding on citizenship. The second sentence's references to "privileges or immunities" and "due process of law" were intended to require states to observe the federal Bill of Rights, and largely did so after a century of judicial wandering in the desert.[163] This change was so thorough that few today remember there was a time when states could establish taxpayer-supported churches (as some did through the early 19th century), could suppress freedom of speech and press (as many pro-slavery states did), and could use the products of coerced confessions and unreasonable searches and seizures (allowed until the 1960s).

The election of Abraham Lincoln, arguably our greatest president. Making citizenship universal, regardless of race. Requiring states to observe freedom of religion, of speech, and the other protections of the federal bill of rights. Establishing equal protection of the laws.

Not a bad legacy for Dred and Harriet Scott's quest for freedom.

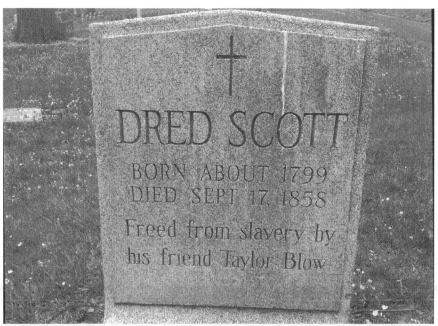

Dred Scott's resting place, Calvary Cemetery, St. Louis

Irene and Calvin Chaffee, Springfield Cemetery, Massachusetts

Epilogue

Dred Scott, unfortunately, did not live to see any of his case's legacy. He died in 1858, only months after securing his family's freedom. The cause of death was attributed to consumption – given the unreliability of 19th century medical diagnoses, it was probably some manner of pulmonary disorder.

Harriet Scott, who was probably the discoverer of the Missouri "freedom suits" and thus the initiator of all the events discussed in this book, at least saw the fruits of her discovery. She continued her work as a laundress, and died in June, 1876. Any historian must lament - she survived their famous case by nearly twenty years, but apart from a few brief press interviews in 1857, no one stopped to gather an oral history from her.

Today, the Scotts' great-great granddaughter, Lynne Jackson, directs the Dred Scott Heritage Foundation, www.dredscottlives.org.

Chief Justice Roger Taney survived until 1864, when he died, still in office, at the age of 87. His reputation had been good prior to *Dred Scott*, but never recovered after it. By the time of his death, the Court was the Taney Court in name only: Lincoln appointed three new Justices in 1862, and one more in 1863. Taney died on the day his state outlawed slavery. Lincoln promptly nominated abolitionist Salmon Chase as his successor.

Henry Taylor Blow. Fate had reserved a special role for Mr. Blow, the friend who supported Dred Scott's litigation and at the end, freed the family. He was elected to the 39th Congress, where he served on the Joint Committee on Reconstruction, which drafted the 14th Amendment that overruled *Dred Scott*. When he died in 1875, his funeral procession was a mile in length.

Major Lawrence Taliaferro, Harriet's initial owner (who married her to Dred, and twice recorded that he had freed her) soldiered on as Indian Agent at Fort Snelling until he resigned in 1839, and retired to Bedford, Pennsylvania. In 1857 he rejoined the Army and served in the Quartermaster's Corps until he retired again in 1863, aged 69. He died in 1871.

John F. A. Sanford, the frontiersman turned millionaire who posed as the Scotts' slaveowner, went insane, possibly from overwork, in 1857. He died in an institution later that year, aged 51.

Dr. Calvin Chaffee lost his seat in the House of Representatives after he lost his re-nomination bid in 1858. Whether the Dred Scott affair affected this is unknown. He faced two challengers, the votes split and deadlocked, whereupon a fourth candidate was proposed. Dr. Chaffee's supporters shifted their votes to the fourth, in order to deprive the first challengers of the nomination, and the fourth candidate won.[164] It is often incorrectly stated (including on Congress's online history of Representatives) that Dr. Chaffee simply chose to retire from politics. He was Librarian of the House of Representatives from 1860 to 1862, thereafter practicing medicine in Washington, D.C. In 1876 he returned to Springfield, Massachusetts, where he died in 1896.

Irene (Sanford/Emerson) Chaffee survived all the other participants in the case, dying in 1903, at the age of 87, having outlived her first husband, Dr. John Emerson, by 60 years. In her later years she gave interviews on the Dred Scott case upon which many historians relied, but which diverged rather sharply from the provable facts.

In these, Scott was shiftless and she had wanted to free the Scott family but was legally powerless to act (in fact she had taken the state freedom suit to the Missouri Supreme Court), and Scott's attorneys had acted out of hopes of collecting money for his back wages (in fact, the Missouri statute on freedom suits forbade the award of back wages).[165]

Montgomery Blair, Dred Scott's primary Supreme Court attorney, supported Lincoln's election and served in Lincoln's cabinet as Postmaster General, where he carried out several reforms of the wartime postal service. He died in 1883.

Roswell Field, the Scotts' St. Louis attorney, continued to practice in that city. He died of cancer in 1869, aged 62. His portraits hang in

Vermont's Windham County Courthouse, where he began the practice of law, and in the St. Louis landmark, the Field House. His son Eugene Field became a prominent children's poet and newspaperman.

Reverdy Johnson, Scott's main opponent in the Supreme Court, supported Union efforts in the Civil War, and was elected to the Senate. There. after some reluctance, he supported the abolition of slavery by the 13th Amendment, but remained a foe of the 14th Amendment.

He died, age 79, after arguing a case in the Maryland Court of Appeals. Leaving dinner at the governor's mansion, he slipped on an icy step, struck his head on the base of a stone pillar, and died instantly from brain injuries.

Additional Reading

Two books on the Scott family, and their court cases, can fairly be described as outstanding:

Don E. Fehrenbacher, *The Dred Scott Case* (1978), which won the Pulitzer Prize in History,

    and

Lea Vandervelde, *Mrs. Dred Scott: A Life on Slavery's Frontier* (2009), which should have won it.

Those interested in the political context of *Dred Scott v. Sandford* will also enjoy Mark A. Graber, *Dred Scott and the Problem of Constitutional Evil* (2006).

Related and useful books are Kenneth C. Kaufman, *Dred Scott's Advocate: A Biography of Roswell M. Field* (1996), James F. Simon, *Lincoln and Chief Justice Taney* (2006), and Carl Brent Swisher, *Roger B. Taney* (1935, reprinted 1961).

About the Author

David T. Hardy has practiced law since 1975, in Tucson, Arizona and in Washington D.C., with the Department of the Interior.

He is admitted to the bar of the United States Supreme Court, the Arizona Supreme Court, the Second and Ninth Circuits, U.S. Courts of Appeals, and to the U.S. District Courts of Arizona, Colorado, and the District of Columbia.

He has published six books and 27 law review articles. One of the latter, *The Original Popular Understanding of the Fourteenth Amendment As Reflected in the Print Media of 1866-1868*, was twice cited by the U.S. Supreme Court in *McDonald v. Chicago*, 561 U.S. 742 (2010). His other articles have been cited in a Supreme Court dissent and by eleven of the thirteen U.S. Circuit Courts of Appeals.

NOTES

[1] *The Trial of the Rev. Jacob Gruber for Inciting Slaves to Insurrection and Rebellion*, AMERICAN STATE TRIALS, vol. 1, p. 69 (John D. Lawson, ed. 1914).

[2] BRIAN MCGINTY, LINCOLN AND THE COURT, p. 197 (2009).

[3] *Ibid.* His wife is also said to have died of a stroke, which was one effect of Yellow Fever.

[4] Thomas E. Carney, *The Political Judge: Justice John McLean's Pursuit of the Presidency,* OHIO HISTORY, vol. 111, p. 124 (2002).

[5] *Ibid.*

[6] http://www.blackpast.org/aah/thomas-james-p-1827-1913

[7] *United States v. Hanway,* No. 15,299 Fed. Cas. 174.

[8] LEA VANDERVELDE, MRS. DRED SCOTT, p. 326 (2009). Prior to this discovery, it had been speculated that the name might have arisen from Scott's mispronunciation of the exclamation "Great Scott!" Apart from the fact that there is no evidence that Dred ever uttered those words, he was identified as Dred long before "Great Scott" became popular in American English, *circa* 1860-1890.

The discovery of his real name undercuts a theory that same Dred was the same person as a slave "Sam," who had been sold by Peter Blow's estate. *See* DON E. FEHRENBACHER, THE DRED SCOTT CASE, pp. 239-40 (1978). The oldest of the Blow children was Peter Ethelred Blow. WALTER EHRLICH, THEY HAVE NO RIGHTS: DRED SCOTT'S STRUGGLE FOR FREEDOM, p. 10 (1979). Given the unusual character of the name, this is suggestive that Dred acquired his name while with the Blow family, not later, and thus is unlikely to have been the Blow family's "Sam."

[9] WALTER EHRLICH, *op. cit.*, p. 183.

[10] DON E. FEHRENBACHER, *op. cit.,* p. 241.

[11] LEA VANDERVELDE, *op. cit.*, p. 75.

[12] AUTO-BIOGRAPHY OF MAJ. LAWRENCE TALIAFERRO, p. 234-35 (1864). Online at https://archive.org/stream/autobiographyofm00talirich/autobiographyofm00talirich_djvu.txt

[13] Taliaferro Papers, Minnesota Historical Society, reel 35.

[14] https://www.climatestations.com/minnesota-weather-history-1820-to-1869/

[15] Charles E. Snyder, *John Emerson, Owner of Dred Scott*, THE ANNALS OF IOWA, vol. 21 pp. 440, 448-49, online at https://ir.uiowa.edu/cgi/viewcontent.cgi?article=6032&context=annals-of-iowa

[16] LEA VANDERVELDE, *op. cit.*, pp. 123-33.

[17] None of the three Seminole Wars ended with a peace treaty. They ended when the United States proclaimed victory and withdrew its troops, leaving the Seminoles where they were.

[18] Illinois Constitution, Art. VI. http://www.idaillinois.org/cdm/ref/collection/isl2/id/167

[19] Act of March 6, 1820, §7. https://www.ourdocuments.gov/doc.php?flash=true&doc=22&page=transcript

[20] In 1857, a Wisconsin newspaper reported that Irene had proposed to sell the Scotts in 1846, and that "this occasioned the instigation of the suit for freedom." MILWAUKEE DAILY NEWS, April 16, 1857, p. 2. But the remoteness, both in distance and in years, from the event being reported makes this report questionable.

[21] National Park Service, *African-American Life in St. Louis, 1804-1865*. Online at https://www.nps.gov/jeff/learn/historyculture/african-american-life-in-saint-louis-1804-through-1865.htm.

[22] https://books.google.com/books?id=4Vct_ZfahXEC&printsec=frontcover&dq=Colored+Aristocracy+of+St.+Louis&hl=en&sa=X&ved=0ahUKEwjRio3s4Z_eAhXnsFQKHUIDBdsQ6AEIKjAA#v=onepage&q=Colored&f=false

[23] At that, St. Louis slavery was not as strange as that of Rome, where slaves might own their own slaves, slavery sometimes took the form of paying a certain percent of one's income to the master, Greek slaves were the most prestigious doctors and quite wealthy, and the wealthier slaves sometimes declined to buy their freedom because the money could be better leveraged elsewhere.

[24] Revised Statutes of the State of Missouri, ch. 69 (1845).

[25] St. Louis Circuit Court Historic Records Project, Freedom Suits Case Files. Online at http://stlcourtrecords.wustl.edu/about-freedom-suits-series.php. *See generally* William E. Foley, *Slave Freedom Suits before Dred Scott*, 79 MO. HISTORICAL REV. p. 1 (1984).

[26] *See Winny v. Whitesides*, 1 Mo. 472 (1824*); Milly v. Smith*, 2 Mo. 36 (1828); *Vincent v. Duncan*, 2 Mo. 214 (1830*); Merry v. Tiffin & Menard*, 1 Mo. 725 (1827); *Julia v. McKinney*, 2 Mo. 270 (1833); *Ralph v. Duncan*, 3 Mo. 194 (1833); *Nat v. Ruddle*, 3 Mo. 400 (1834); *Rachel v. Walker*, 4 Mo. 360 (1836); *Wilson v. Melvin*, 4 Mo. 592 (1837*); Randolph v. Alsey*, 8 Mo. 656 (1844); *Robert v. Melugen*, 9 Mo. 170 (1845) (ruling against petitioner since he failed to prove residence in Illinois with consent of his master).

[27] *The Trial of the Action of Dred Scott (a Slave) against Irene Emerson for False Imprisonment and Assault,* AMERICAN STATE TRIALS, vol. 13, pp. 220, 225. (John D. Lawson, ed. 1921).

[28] Missouri Revised Statutes, Ch. 69 §9 (1845).

[29] *See* David Thomas Konig, *The Long Road to* Dred Scott: *Personhood and the Rule of Law in the Trial Court Records of St. Louis Slave Freedom Suits*, UMKC LAW REV., vol. 75, pp. 57, 67 (2006). Bates is an interesting historical figure. He (1) was a slaveowner; (2) filed freedom suits on behalf of alleged slaves, and (3) as Attorney General refused to follow *Dred Scott*, ruling that black Americans were citizens. *See id.* at 72; Dennis K. Boman, *The Dred Scott Case Reconsidered: The Legal and Political Context in Missouri,* AMER. J. LEGAL HISTORY. Vol. 44, pp. 405, 415 (2000).

[30] OPINION OF ATTORNEY GENERAL BATES ON CITIZENSHIP, p. 24 (1862). The earlier Missouri statute is online at https://www.sos.mo.gov/CMSImages/MDH/1807FreedomStatute.pdf.

[31] The author recalls reading a medical journal of the 1870s, which noted that since it publishes all the obituaries of doctors in the state, it could calculate their median age at death to be 54.5.

[32] *The Trial of the Action of Dred Scott (a Slave) against Irene Emerson for False Imprisonment and Assault,* AMERICAN STATE TRIALS, vol. 13, p, 228. (John D. Lawson, ed. 1921).

[33] *Scott (a man of color) v. Emerson*, 15 Mo. 576, 577 (1852). The Missouri opinion is online at http://digital.wustl.edu/cgi/t/text/pageviewer-idx?c=dre&cc=dre&idno=dre1852.0088.090&frm=frameset&view=image&seq=1

[34] 98 Eng. Rep. 499 (King's Bench 1772).

[35] 166 Eng. Rep. 179 (Admiralty 1822).

[36] 15 Mo., pp. 576, 584 (1852).

[37] 15 Mo., p. 586.

[38] St. Louis Land Records, Book Y-4, pages 446-47.

[39] Springfield, Massachusetts marriage records, obtained via Ancestry.com.

[40] W. V. N. Bay, *George W. Goode* in REMINISCENCES OF THE BENCH AND BAR OF ST. LOUIS, p. 570 (1878).

[41] *See generally* SHIRLEY CHRISTIAN, BEFORE LEWIS AND CLARK: THE STORY OF THE CHOUTEAUS, THE FRENCH DYNASTY THAT RULED AMERICA'S FRONTIER (2004).

[42] Janet Lecompte, *Pierre Chouteau*, in MOUNTAIN MEN AND FUR TRADERS OF THE FAR WEST pp. 52-54 (LeRoy Hagen, ed. 1982).

[43] National Park Service, "Suits for Freedom," online at https://www.nps.gov/jeff/learn/historyculture/loader.cfm?csModule=security/getfile&PageID=3120182

[44] *Charlotte (of color) v. Chouteau*, 9 Mo. 194 (1847); *Pierre (of color) v. Chouteau*, 9 Mo. 3 (1847).

[45] *Mrs. Chaffee, Owner of the Old Slave, Still Living in Springfield,* NEW YORK TIMES, December 22, 1895.

[46] DON E. FEHRENBACHER, *op. cit.*, p. 270

[47] The Judiciary Act of 1789 gave federal courts no original jurisdiction (ability to open and try cases) on federal questions. Federal questions had to be handled by raising them in state court, taking an appeal to the highest state court, and then appealing that result to the U.S. Supreme Court. *An Act to Establish the Judicial Court of the United States*, 1 Stat. 73, §25. Even after the Civil War, and the passage of postwar civil rights acts, original jurisdiction of Federal questions was considerably narrower than it is today. *See* Revised Statutes of the United States (2d Ed.) Tit. 13, §§ 3, 13, 15, 16, 17, 18 (1878).

[48] DON E. FEHRENBACHER, *op. cit.*, p. 276 The court which tried the case will be identified simply as the "trial court." It was the federal Circuit Court, but that designation is confusing to modern lawyers, to whom a federal Circuit Court is a court of appeals, not a trial court. Under the Judiciary Act of 1789, a circuit court (often though not always including a Supreme Court justice "riding circuit" to visit courts within his assigned area) had some appellate duties but also tried the more important cases within its jurisdiction.

[49] National Archives, Dred Scott v. Sanford file.

[50] E-mail to author from Suzanne Christoff, Associate Director for Unique Resources, U.S. Military Academy Library, dated April 26, 2012.

[51] The text of the treaty with Kansa can be found at http://resources.utulsa.edu/law/classes/rice/Treaties/07_Stat_244_KANSA.htm

[52] John Francis Alexander Sanford, online at https://www.geni.com/people/John-Sanford/6000000026027824236

[53] Janet Lecompte, *Pierre Chouteau, Jr*, in MOUNTAIN MEN AND FUR TRADERS OF THE FAR WEST (LeRoy R. Hafen, ed. 1982), pp. 40, 47.

[54] *The Illinois Central Railroad*, DAILY ILLINOIS STATE JOURNAL, April 23, 1853, p. 2.

[55] 1 THOMAS J. SCHARF, HISTORY OF SAINT LOUIS CITY AND COUNTY, FROM THE EARLIEST PERIODS TO THE PRESENT DAY p. 183 (1883).

[56] PHILADELPHIA INQUIRER, May 16, 1857, p. 2.

[57] Susan Bainbridge Hay, The Egotistigraphy by John Sanford Barnes, Internet Edition. Online at https://sites.google.com/site/johnsanfordbarnes/home

[58] *Died*, ALBANY EVENING JOURNAL, May 11, 1857, p. 3.

[59] *Dred Scott v. Sandford*, 60 U.S., p. 398.

[60] Letter from Roswell Field to Montgomery Blair, dated January 7, 1855, Library of Congress, Manuscript Division, Blair Family Papers.

[61] Charles E. Snyder, *op. cit.*, p. 456.

[62] WALTER EHRLICHT, *op. cit.*, p. 39.

[63] F. H. Hodder, *Some Phases of the Dred Scott Case*, MISS. VALLEY HIST. REV., vol. 16, pp. 3, 5 (1929).

[64] Deed from Eliza Irene Emerson to Alfred Vinton, recorded March 29, 1849. City of St. Louis Recorder of Deeds, book Y-4, pages 446-47. It is noteworthy that Irene signed in her individual capacity, suggesting that the probate was closed by the time of the deed. If had not been, then the executor of Dr. Emerson's estate should have made the contract.

[65] DON E. FEHRENBACHER, *op. cit.*, pp. 275-76.

[66] So called because it tended to be secretive, and members were said to be instructed that, if asked about the party's internal affairs, they were to say that they knew nothing.

[67] *Served two terms in Congress*, BOSTON HERALD, August 8, 1896, p. 3.

[68] *Ex-Congressman Chaffee Dead*, SPRINGFIELD REPUBLICAN, August 10, 1896, p. 10.

[69] Susan Bainbridge Hay, *The Egotistigraphy by John Sanford Barnes, Internet Edition.* Online at https://sites.google.com/site/johnsanfordbarnes/home. The original of Barnes' work is in the Naval Collection of the New York Historical Society.

[70] "Dr. Chaffee was called, sewed up the wound and Prince was soon about again." *Ibid.*, Ch. 1.

[71] *Ibid.*

[72] Dred Scott case file, National Archives. Also online at https://www.loc.gov/resource/llst.081/?sp=1

The Marshal's affidavit of service is interesting in that he says he served Sanford "by offering to read a copy of the same," and that Sanford "declined hearing, and asked for a copy of said declaration [the complaint], which I furnished him." The procedure likely required an offer to read the documents since in 1857 it could not be assumed that every defendant was literate.

[73] HAROLD HOLZER, LINCOLN AT COOPER UNION, pp. 63, 64, 206 (2004).

[74] From slave states: Chief Justice Taney was from Maryland; Justices Wayne and Campbell from Georgia; Justice Daniel from Virginia; and Justice Catron from Tennessee.

From free states: Justice Nelson hailed from New York; Justice Grier from Pennsylvania; Justice Curtis from Massachusetts; and Justice McLean from Ohio.

[75] MARK A. GRABER, DRED SCOTT AND THE PROBLEM OF CONSTITUTIONAL EVIL, p. 37 (2006).

[76] PAUL FINKELMAN, DRED SCOTT V. SANDFORD: A BRIEF HISTORY WITH DOCUMENTS, p. 30 (1997).

[77] *Ibid.*, p. 29.

[78] 51 U.S. 82 (1850). *Strader* involved a civil suit for damages against a steamboat owner who had carried escaping slaves. He defended on the ground that their master had sent them for long periods into a free state, making them free. Thus, the steamboat owner had not aided slaves in their escape. The Supreme Court ruled that no federal issue was presented, since the slaves' status was determined by state law, and they were thus returned to slavery when they returned to the slave state.

[79] Dred Scott v. Irene Emerson, 24 St. Louis Circuit Court Record 33 (Jan. 25th, 1854), online at
http://digital.wustl.edu/cgi/t/text/text-idx?c=dre;cc=dre;view=text;idno=dre1854.0100.102;rgn=div1;node=dre1854.0100.102%3A1

[80] Letter from Roswell Field to Montgomery Blair, Mar, 12, 1856. Library of Congress, Manuscript Division, Blair Family Papers.

[81] It must be understood that in the 19th century, and into more modern times, engagement was a very serious matter, and a person could be sued for "breach of promise to marry." In his younger days, *circa* 1971, the author helped to defend against such a suit, which the state legislature later abolished by statute.

[82] KENNETH C. KAUFMAN, DRED SCOTT'S ADVOCATE: A BIOGRAPHY OF ROSWELL M. FIELD, pp. 56-70 (1996).

[83] WALTER EHRLICH, *op. cit.*, p. 95. In disposing of his state freedom suit appeal, the Missouri Supreme Court had privately considered ruling against the Missouri Compromise, even though counsel had not made that argument. After Justice Napton lost his bid for re-election, the issue was never taken up. Diary of Judge Napton, p. 223, Napton and Dred Scott Collections, Missouri Historical Society.

[84] Roswell Field letter to Montgomery Blair, Dec. 24, 1854, Library of Congress, Manuscript Division, Blair Family Papers.

[85] Field did not discuss the question of citizenship, probably because he had won that issue at trial and felt Sanford had waived the appeal, under the common law rules of pleading, by "pleading over" and proceeding to trial. In modern practice, there is no inconsistency in moving to dismiss because the court lacks jurisdiction and in going to trial and appealing the trial result. In common law pleading it was more complex, and a defendant might be put to the dilemma of moving to dismiss, or objecting to the outcome of the trial, but not doing both.

[86] Plea to the Jurisdiction of the Court, Dred Scott case file, National Archives. A printed version submitted to the Supreme Court is online at https://www.loc.gov/resource/llst.081/?sp=1.

[87] See *Bank of Augusta v. Earle*, 38 U.S. 519, 528-29 (1839); *Louisville, Cincinnati & Charleston Ry. Co. v. Letson*, 43 U.S. 497, 555 (1844) ("A corporation ... seems to us to be a person, though an artificial one, inhabiting and belonging to that state, and therefore entitled, for the purpose of suing and being sued, to be deemed a citizen of that state."); *Ohio & Miss. RR Co. v. Wheeler*, 66 U.S. 286, 296 (1861) ("[A] suit by or against a corporation in its corporate name must be presumed to be a suit by or against citizens of the state which created the corporate body, and that no averment or evidence to the contrary is admissible for the purposes of withdrawing the suit from the jurisdiction of a court of the United States.").

[88] Plea of Defendant, Dred Scott case file, National Archives.

[89] *Dred Scott v. Sandford*, 60 U.S. at p. 399.

[90] Verdict, Dred Scott case file, National Archives.

[91] For reasons never explained, the petition for a writ of error, then the first document in a Supreme Court appeal, was signed by Nathaniel Holmes, a St. Louis attorney who made no other appearance in the case.

[92] DON E. FEHRENBACHER, *op. cit.*, p. 280, citing a copy of the May 18, 1854 *St. Louis Morning Herald*.

[93] *The Trial of the Action of Dred Scott (a Slave) against Irene Emerson for False Imprisonment and Assault*, AMERICAN STATE TRIALS, vol. 13, pp. 243-44. (John D. Lawson, ed. 1921).

[94] Kenneth C. Kaufman, *op. cit.*, p. 200.

[95] *Brown v. Maryland*, 25 U.S. 419 (1827).

[96] DRED SCOTT, A COLORED MAN VS. JOHN F. A. SANFORD: ARGUMENT OF MONTGOMERY BLAIR, OF COUNSEL FOR THE PLAINTIFF IN ERROR 26-40 (n.d.).

[97] *See Important from Washington*, NEW YORK HERALD, Jan. 1, 1857, at 4 (reporting that Court will rule 7-2 that Congress has no power over slavery in the territories); *By Telegraph*, ALBANY EVENING JOURNAL, Jan. 8, 1857 (same: Taney will write the decision); *The Dred Scott Case*, NEW YORK TIMES, Feb. 5, 1857 (reporting that the Washington UNION states vote will be 7-2, Curtis and McLean dissenting, but discounting the report since it would be "unusual" for a ruling to "leak out in advance.").

[98] Letter from Montgomery Blair to Martin van Buren, Feb. 5, 1857, Martin van Buren Papers, Library of Congress Manuscript Division, reel 33.

[99] https://www.presidency.ucsb.edu/documents/inaugural-address-33

[100] Cong. Globe, 35th Cong., 1st Sess., p. 941.

[101] SAMUEL TYLER, MEMOIR OF ROGER BROOKE TANEY p. 391 (n.d.). ("In such abhorrence did Chief-Justice Taney hold the conduct of Mr. Seward, in so wantonly assailing the Supreme Court, that he told me, if Mr. Seward had been nominated and elected President instead of Mr. Lincoln, he should, if requested, as was customary, have refused to administer to him the official oath, and thereby proclaim to the nation that he would not administer that oath to such a man.").

[102] The best compilation of the letters is Philip Auchampaugh, *James Buchanan, The Court, and the Dred Scott Case*, TENNESSEE HISTORICAL MAGAZINE, vol. 9, p. 231 (1926), online at https://www.jstor.org/stable/42638039?read-now=1&loggedin=true&seq=9#metadata_info_tab_contents. Some of the letters are reprinted in JOHN BASSETT MOORE, THE WORKS OF JAMES BUCHANAN, vol. 10, p. 106-07 n. 1 (1910); and in BERNARD C. STEINER, LIFE OF ROGER BROOKE TANEY 338-40 (1922). The reason why Buchanan's letters are missing is simple. Before the invention of carbon paper and photocopiers, keeping copies of your own correspondence required copying it by hand, which few were willing to do. As a result, collections of a person's papers tended to consist of many letters to, and few letters from, him. Buchanan did a better job of preserving his papers than did the Justices.

[103] The "Nicholson letter" was an 1847 letter from Sen. Lewis Cass, to A. P. Nicholson, arguing that Congress did not have general power to regulate slavery in the territories, but that territorial government did.

[104] Of the four free state Justices, Nelson was not going to reach the Missouri Compromise issue, and Curtis and McLean were going to vote to uphold it. If Grier joined with any of these Justices, the result would be a 5-4 split along slave state – free state lines.

[105] Both, *i.e.*, Scott's citizenship and the constitutionality of the Missouri Compromise. Nelson would have written an opinion that disposed of the case by finding that when the Scotts returned to Missouri they reverted to slavery under Missouri law.

[106] *The Trial of the Rev. Jacob Gruber for Inciting Slaves to Insurrection and Rebellion*, AMERICAN STATE TRIALS, vol. 1, p. 89 (John D. Lawson, ed. 1914).

[107] Law of June 7, 1806, online at https://www.accessible-archives.com/2011/08/the-black-code-of-louisiana-1806/

[108] Curtis E. Gannon & Ross E. Davies, *B. R. & G. T. Curtis*, GREEN BAG 2D vol. 10, p. 207, 237 (2007).

[109] *Ibid.*, p. 237.

[110] MACON TELEGRAPH, April 7, 1857, p. 2.

[111] Curtis E. Gannon & Ross E. Davies, *op. cit.* p. 228.

[112] *Ibid.*, p. 234.

[113] MACON TELEGRAPH, April 7, 1857, p. 2 ("copies of the same [the dissents] had been previously furnished for the press...."); RICHLAND OBSERVER (WI), April 21, 1857, p. 2 (The dissenters had "publish[ed] their Opinions, in advance of filing them...").

[114] *See generally* MARK A. GRABER, DRED SCOTT AND THE PROBLEM OF CONSTITUTIONAL EVIL (2006).

[115] I am not being anachronistic here: as will be seen, Chaffee later admitted that he knew about his wife's ownership prior to the ruling.

[116] "The *Springfield Argus,* which has been published daily and weekly about two years by Elon Comstock, Esq., has been discontinued. – The recent financial difficulties are stated as the cause of the suspension." PITTSFIELD SUN (MA), Dec. 3, 1857, p. 2. Only the issue of February 6, 1856 survives. GREGORY WINIFRED GEROULD & GERTRUDE CLARKE AVIS, UNION LIST OF AMERICAN NEWSPAPERS 1821-1936, p. 299 (1967). That issue is in the possession of the American Antiquarian Society in Springfield, Massachusetts. The Wood Museum of Springfield History has no copies of the *Argus.* Email from Margaret Humberston of the Wood Museum, to the author, June 15, 2012.

[117] *Dred Scott Owned by a Republican Member of Congress*, SYRACUSE DAILY COURIER, March 17, 1857, p. 2.

[118] *Dred Scott and his "Republican" Owner*, SYRACUSE DAILY COURIER, May 30, 1857, p. 2.

[119] *Ibid.*

[120] *Interesting*, PITTSFIELD SUN (MA), March 19, 1857, p. 2.

[121] DAILY PHAROS (Logansport, IL) Aug. 18, 1858, p. 5.

[122] HAROLD HOLZER, ED., THE LINCOLN DOUGLAS DEBATES, pp. 212-13 (1993) (Debate at Charlestown: "[T]here were no Democratic owners of Dred Scott in this land. He was owned at the time by Rev. Dr. Chaffee, an abolition member of Congress from Springfield, and his wife."), pp. 296-97 (Debate in Quincy: "Dred Scott was at the time owned by Rev. Dr. Chaffee, an abolition member of Congress from Springfield, Massachusetts, in right of his wife, and hence he was owned by one of Lincoln's friends, and not by Democrats at all.").

[123] *Dred Scott – Who is His Owner – Dr. Chaffee*, SPRINGFIELD REPUBLICAN, Mar, 14, 1857, p. 4.

[124] *The Wish Father to the Thought*, LOWELL DAILY CITIZEN AND NEWS (MA), Mar. 16, 1857, p. 2.

[125] *Dred Scott and Hon C. C. Chaffee*, NEW YORK DAILY TRIBUNE, March 17, 1857 p. 5. Other newspapers carried shorter forms of Chaffee's defense. *See* BOSTON HERALD, March 17, 1857 p. 2; *Slow Coaches*, LOWELL DAILY CITIZEN AND NEWS (MA), March 19, 1857, p. 2.

[126] NEW YORK HERALD TRIBUNE, June 6, 1857 p. 4. The claims that Mrs. Chaffee had left Scott to his own devices since Dr. Emerson's death is not consistent with the evidence. Dr. Emerson died in 1843. The State suits for freedom, in which the evidence indicated that when Scott was "hired out" the funds went to Mrs. Emerson/Chaffee, occupied 1846-1852. We may suspect that the *Tribune* confused two events. It is likely that Mrs. Chaffee left Scott to his own devices after she moved to Massachusetts in 1850 and married Dr. Chaffee. Scott's ownership would have been awkward to mention to a potential mate who was an abolitionist. The Scotts would have been happy to be left alone. The state freedom suit's being "left on the back burner" for years after its remand to the trial court would be consistent with her attorney having received no instructions to proceed.

[127] *Dr. Chaffee and Dred Scott*, PIITSFIELD SUN (MA), April 2, 1857 p. 3.

[128] MILWAUKEE DAILY NEWS, April 16, 1857, p. 2.

[129] *The Question Repeated*, PITTSFIELD SUN, May 14, 1857, p. 2.

[130] Letter from Calvin Chaffee to Montgomery Blair, April 1, 1857, Blair Family Papers, Dred Scott folder, Manuscript Division, Library of Congress [hereinafter Blair Family Papers].

[131] Letter from Calvin Chaffee to Montgomery Blair, April 11, 1857, Blair Family Papers.

[132] Letter from Roswell Field to Montgomery Blair, April 29, 1857. Blair Family Papers. Some historians have assumed the transfer to Blow was necessary since only a Missouri resident could free Missouri slaves. Field's letter makes clear the real reason: the person freeing the slaves must appear in open court, and it was far easier to deed the Scotts to a local resident than for the Chaffees to travel to St. Louis.

[133] *Id.* Catron had voted with the majority, holding that Dred Scott remained a slave.

[134] Letter from Calvin Chaffee to Montgomery Blair, May 6, 1857. Blair Family Papers. ("My wife is now in N.Y. being summoned by the fatal illness of her Br. J. F. A. Sanford the deft. of the suit which has made humanity grieve and all true Americans blush – Mr. Sanford died yesterday at 12 M. I suppose of congestion of the brain. My wife will remain there till Saturday & I hope next week to get the papers executed, of which I will apprise you.")

[135] Letter of Calvin Chaffee to Montgomery Blair, May 14, 1857. Blair Family Papers. Dr. Chaffee's hoped in vain to keep the emancipation secret. Within a week Missouri newspapers were reporting the event. *Dred Scott Free*, HANNIBAL MESSENGER, June 2, 1857, p. 2 (citing a story in the St. Louis News).

[136] ALLAN NEVINS, op. cit., vol. 1, p. 96.

[137] JOHN G. NICOLAY & JOHN HAY, ABRAHAM LINCOLN: A HISTORY, vol. 2, p. 58 (1914).

[138] Typescript copy of unsigned letter dated February 11, 1907, Missouri Historical Society's Dred Scott collection.

[139] *The Dred Scott Decision*, NEW YORK TIMES, August 15, 1857.

[140] NEW YORK DAILY TRIBUNE, April 1, 1857, p. 4.

[141] MADISON DAILY STATE JOURNAL, March 17, 1857, p. 2.

[142] FAIRFIELD LEDGER, March 26, 1857 p. 3.

[143] MADISON DAILY STATE JOURNAL, April 27, 1857, p. 2.

[144] PAUL FINKELMAN, op. cit., p. 183. This is a bit of an overstatement: Lincoln had unsuccessfully run for the vice presidency at the 1856 Republican convention. But at the time of the ruling, Lincoln was not yet a Senate candidate. The Cooper Union speech, which made Lincoln into a national figure, would not come until nearly three years after *Dred Scott.*

[145] 3 JOHN G. NICOLAY & JOHN HAY, COMPLETE WORKS OF ABRAHAM LINCOLN vol. 3, pp. 2-3, 9-10 (1905).

[146] *Extracts from the Speech of Senator Trumbull*, OLNEY TIMES (Il) August 27, 1858, p. 1.

[147] PITTSFIELD BERKSHIRE COUNTY EAGLE, October 15, 1858, p. 2.

[148] JAMES F. SIMON, LINCOLN AND CHIEF JUSTICE TANEY, pp. 136-39 (2006).

[149] HAROLD HOLZER, *op. cit.*, p. 76.

[150] *Ibid.*, pp. 54, 76, 70, 71, 74-76, 101-02, 107-09, 124-25, 151, 153, 168-73, 169-71, 212-13, 223, 226, 262-65, 285-87, 295, 296, 249, 303, 315-16, 320, 325, 341-42, 360, 361-62.

[151] HAROLD HOLZER, LINCOLN AT COOPER UNION, p. 263 (2004).

[152] *Ibid.*, pp. 157-58.

[153] *Ibid.*, p. 149.

[154] *Ibid.*, p. 235.

[155] *See* PAUL FINKELMAN, *op. cit.*, pp. 213-15.

[156] HAROLD HOLZER, THE LINCOLN-DOUGLAS DEBATES, p. 96 (1993). The transcript of the question has "the United States territory." I think it more likely that Lincoln used "a United States territory" and have used that.

[157] *Ibid.*, p. 106.

[158] It should be mentioned that Douglas' approach was not the only one that could be taken: in fact it ran contrary to the pro-slavery position, which was that slaves were ordinary property, and thus could be held anywhere unless prohibited by legislation. That is, on the slave vs. free issue, slavery was the default answer. The Missouri Supreme Court took this position in *Charlotte (of color) v. Chouteau*, 9 Mo. 195 (1847), where it rejected a freedom suit that was based on the plaintiff's mother having been born in Canada. The court noted that the absence of slaves in Canada might be due to the climate. "But if negro slavery was introduced into that country in fact, although to a very limited extent, without meeting any opposition from the positive laws or established usages … the defendant's rights, acquired in such a condition of things, deserve the protection of our laws and courts…." That is, Canada might be a "slave country" if its laws neither allowed or forbade slavery. Or, as a pro-slavery writer put it, "Slavery exists, actually or in theory, wherever in the states of this Union it has not been abolished by the decree of some competent authority. It is free-soil that does not exist and cannot exist, except by legislation." *Squatter Sovereignty*, THE WEEKLY BRUNSWICKER (MD), April 5, 1856, p. 2.

[159] JOHN G. NICOLAY & JOHN HAY, ABRAHAM LINCOLN: A HISTORY, vol. 2, p. 84 (1914).

[160] See http://www.ushist.com/general-information/1860_national_presidential_election_platforms.shtml

[161] HAROLD HOLZER, *op. cit.*, p. 23.

[162] F. H. Hodder, *op. cit.,* p. 21.

[163] To shorten a long story, in the 1870s the Supreme Court held that the privileges and immunities clause did not require states to observe the federal bill of rights; over a period spanning the 1890s to the present, the Supreme Court held that the due process clause required states to observe almost all of that bill of rights, with the Court deciding which guarantees would apply to the states. As this book goes to press, the Supreme Court is considering whether the "excessive fines" prohibition of the 8th Amendment applies to the states.

[164] SPRINGFIELD REPUBLICAN, September 25, 1858, p. 4.

[165] Missouri Revised Statutes, Ch. 69, §14 (1845).

Made in the USA
Columbia, SC
07 December 2019